# AD410
## THE YEAR
## THAT SHOOK
# ROME

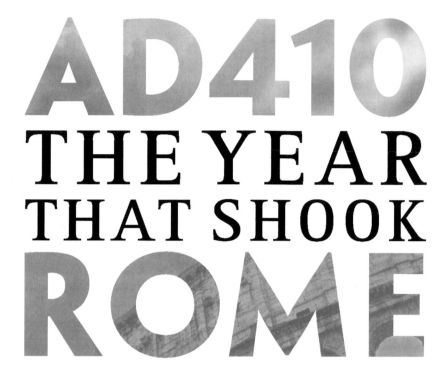

# AD410
# THE YEAR
# THAT SHOOK
# ROME

SAM MOORHEAD & DAVID STUTTARD

THE BRITISH MUSEUM PRESS

To Fi and EJ

*Frontispiece*
Sculptural relief depicting the Battle of the Milvian Bridge, 312,
from the Arch of Constantine, Rome, 315.

© 2010 Sam Moorhead and David Stuttard

First published in 2010 by The British Museum Press
A division of The British Museum Company Ltd
38 Russell Square, London, WC1B 3QQ

Sam Moorhead and David Stuttard have asserted
their right to be identified as the authors of this work.

A catalogue record of this book is available
from the British Library

ISBN 978 0 7141 2269 4

Designed by John Hawkins
Printed in Hong Kong

# Contents

| | | |
|---|---|---|
| Acknowledgements | | 6 |
| Dramatis personae | | 8 |

*Prologue*
|   | Preface | 12 |
|---|---|---|
| 1 | Rome, eternal city | 16 |

*Part 1  A house divided*
|   |   |   |
|---|---|---|
| 2 | A new world order | 30 |
| 3 | Rome baptized | 39 |

*Part 2  The storm clouds gather*
|   |   |   |
|---|---|---|
| 4 | Stirrings on the steppes | 54 |
| 5 | Stilicho ascendant | 67 |
| 6 | Implosion | 79 |

*Part 3  The sack of Rome*
|   |   |   |
|---|---|---|
| 7 | Rome besieged | 92 |
| 8 | Impotent emperors | 103 |
| 9 | Barbarian puppets | 115 |
| 10 | Rome taken | 124 |

*Epilogue*
|    |   |   |
|----|---|---|
| 11 | Shockwaves | 138 |

| | |
|---|---|
| Aftermath: Rome AD 410–575 | 151 |
| Who's Who in AD 410 | 153 |
| Original sources | 163 |
| Further reading | 169 |
| Endnotes | 171 |
| Timeline 753 BC–AD 711 | 175 |
| Maps | 179 |
| Index | 182 |
| Picture credits | 184 |

# Acknowledgements

Our association and collaboration stretches back well before the inception of this book to long and stimulating evening conversations on the Mediterranean and Aegean, when we were both, in our different ways, serving as the grist to the mill of Swan Hellenic cruises. We thank that organization for these opportunities and for bringing us together.

Since then, we have worked on numerous projects, many of them in association with the British Museum. It was Nina Shandloff who first championed this book, and we are grateful to her and to Rosemary Bradley, Director of Publishing at the British Museum Press, for setting it so firmly on track; to Axelle Russo for ensuring it was so vividly illustrated; to Jerry Fowler for his clear and detailed maps; to Victoria Benjamin for promoting it so energetically; to John Hawkins and Bobby Birchall for their inspirational design; and, above all, to our editor, Belinda Wilkinson, for her unwavering support and encouragement, her attention to detail (of which Diocletian himself would have been proud) and the mastery with which she curbed our wilder excesses.

We have been grateful, too, to other colleagues for their advice and comments: at the British Museum, to Lesley Fitton, Paul Roberts, Richard Abdy, Richard Woff and Ralph Jackson, who have all, in their different ways, been valued sounding-boards, and provided useful insights; to Fiona Haarer of the Roman Society; Fernando López Sánchez at Oxford; and the librarians at the Institute of Classical Studies, who helped track down texts.

Many vibrant images illustrate the narrative, and we are particularly grateful to Eleanor Ghey and Kris Lockyear for scenes of the Danube, and to the British Museum's Department of Photography and Imaging for providing a wealth of evocative images, including many new photographs of ancient art, artefacts and treasures – the majority drawn from the Museum's own extensive collection.

Many of these colleagues were kind enough to read the book in manuscript, as were Ken Dark, Neil Faulkner, Giles Cooley, Ian Angus Wilkie, Miren Lopategni and Kate Stuttard. We owe a debt of gratitude to them all for their perceptive observations and advice. Any shortcomings that remain in the text are entirely our own responsibility.

Finally, we would like to thank Margaret and Gordon Tomlinson, residents of Ostia, for their warm hospitality and the meticulously arranged itinerary, which ensured that our research trip to Rome and Ravenna went so smoothly. Had the Roman Empire been in such safe hands in AD 410, history might yet have been changed.

But more than anyone, thank you to our respective partners, Fi and Emily-Jane, who, for the best part of six months, stoically endured our lives being consumed by Alaric, Honorius and the rest, and whose support, good sense and humour all contributed to easing the work's transition from pencilled scratchings to finished book.

Sam Moorhead and David Stuttard
*September 2009*

# Dramatis personae

*Fuller character sketches appear in the 'Who's Who in AD 410', on pp. 153–62, and the 'Original sources', on pp. 163–8.*

## Romans

**Ambrose, St** (d. 397) bishop of Milan who opposed Symmachus and Theodosius I.

**Arcadius** (r. 395–408) emperor of the eastern empire; son of Theodosius I.

**Augustine, St** (354–430) bishop of Hippo Regius in North Africa and theologian who tried to rationalize the sack of Rome for Christians.

**Constantine I** (r. 306–37) first Christian emperor of the Roman Empire; founded Constantinople.

**Constantine III** (r. 407–11) rival emperor to Honorius, who ruled in the northwest of the Roman Empire.

**Constantius III** (r. 421) successful general of Honorius before reigning briefly as emperor; husband to Galla Placidia and father of Valentinian III.

**Diocletian** (r. 284–305) emperor who reformed the Roman Empire after the troubles of the third century.

**Eucherius** (d. 408) son of Stilicho; betrothed to Galla Placidia.

**Eudoxia** (d. 404) wife of Arcadius.

**Eutropius** (d. *c.*400) eunuch and leading minister in the court of Arcadius.

**Galerius** (r. 293–311) emperor who was a zealous persecutor of Christians.

**Galla Placidia** (*c.*388-450) daughter of Theodosius I; betrothed to Eucherius; married to Ataulf and Constantius III; mother of Valentinian III and the power behind his throne

**Heraclian** (d. 413) responsible for the execution of Stilicho; rewarded by Honorius with command of North Africa; executed after a failed rebellion against Honorius.

**Honorius** (r. 395–423) son of Theodosius and ruler of the western empire; ineffective emperor who spent most of his time at Ravenna while Stilicho and other ministers attempted to save the empire.

**Innocent I** (r. 402–17) pope who played an important role in negotiations between Alaric and Honorius.

**Jerome, St** (*c.*342–420) Christian writer and translator of the Bible into Latin.

**Jovius** (*fl.* early 400s) mercurial character who served under Stilicho, Honorius and Priscus Attalus and was a friend of Alaric.

**Marcella** (325–410) noble Roman lady who founded an early form of convent on the Aventine Hill; died during the sack of Rome in 410.

**Maria** (d. 407) eldest daughter of Stilicho and first wife of Honorius.

**Olympius** (d. *c.*?411–15); promoted by Stilicho, but turned against him and became a leading minister for Honorius.

**Palladius** (d. 421) junior senator responsible for raising funds to pay Alaric's ransom demands in 408.

**Priscus Attalus** (r. 409–10 and 414–5) made emperor by Alaric in 409, but deposed by Alaric in 410; remained in the court of Ataulf and briefly became emperor again in Gaul in 414–5.

**Rufinus** (d. 395) briefly ran the eastern empire for Arcadius before being assassinated.

**Serena** (d. 408) niece of Theodosius I and wife of Stilicho; executed in Rome.

**Stilicho** (d. 408) half-Roman, half-Vandal general who served under Theodosius and effectively ran the western empire for Honorius; defeated Alaric, but attempted to accommodate him, partly leading to his downfall.

**Symmachus** (*c.*340–402) leading Roman senator who attempted to preserve paganism.

**Theodosius I** (r. 379–95) emperor who saved the empire from destruction after the Battle of Hadrianople in 378; banned all pagan practices in 391; and split the empire between his sons, Arcadius and Honorius.

**Theodosius II** (r. 402–50) son of Arcadius and emperor of the east, most famed for the Theodosian Walls of Constantinople

**Thermantia** (d. 415) daughter of Stilicho and second wife of Honorius.

**Valens** (r. 364–78) emperor who failed to check the Visigothic invasion of the empire, and died with most of his army at the Battle of Hadrianople.

**Valens** (d. 410) general who served under Honorius and Priscus Attalus before being executed by Alaric.

**Valentinian III** (r. 425–55) emperor of the west; son of Galla Placidia and Constantius III.

## Barbarians

**Alaric** (r. 395–410/11) king of the Visigoths who sacked Rome in 410.

**Arbogast** (d. 394) Frankish general in the service of Rome; made Eugenius emperor.

**Ataulf** (r. 411–15) king of the Visigoths and brother-in-law of Alaric.

**Attila** (d. 453) king of the Huns at the height of their power.

**Fritigern** (d. *c.*380) Visigothic king who led his people into the empire in 376 and won the Battle of Hadrianople in 378.

**Generid** (*fl.* early 400s) barbarian general who served under Honorius.

**Gainas** (d. 400/1) Gothic general in service of the eastern empire, who killed Rufinus and later rebelled.

**Odovacer** (r. 476–493) king in Italy who deposed the last Roman emperor of the west, Romulus Augustulus, but acknowledged the authority of the eastern empire.

**Radagaisus** (d. 406) Ostrogothic king who invaded the empire more than once; defeated and killed by Stilicho.

**Sarus** (d. *c.*412) Visigothic general who apparently fell out with Alaric and Ataulf and served Honorius.

**Theodoric the Ostrogoth** (r. 493–526) king of Italy who maintained much of the Roman way of life in Ravenna and Rome.

*A cockerel was scratching around for something for his family to eat, when he came across a precious jewel. And he cried out: 'I'm sure you're a great treasure to all who value you, but I'd rather have one grain of corn than all the jewels in the world!'*
(Aesop)

# Prologue

# Preface

Rome in the early hours of 24 August AD 410... No eyewitness account survives, nor is it likely – in the aftermath of that night's events – that such an account was ever written. But from the letters, histories and soul-searching analyses of the people who lived through the times, we can still catch tantalizing glimpses of the drama that unfolded on that summer's night, and of the lives of those caught up in it.

We hear of Proba, the rich matriarch, with her crates and cases already packed for a swift escape by sea; and the eighty-five-year-old Marcella, who long before had turned her palace, high above the Tiber, into a sanctuary for fellow Christian women. We hear of senators, still clinging to the myth of Rome's supremacy, still harbouring resentments that their colleagues had sold out to the barbarians. And we know, too, of countless others – the entire poor of Rome – their private feelings unrecorded, but all together caught up in the turmoil of that night; their ears attuned to what they all feared most: the distant rasp of splintering wood, the pound of rushing feet, the war-cries and the screams, the ghastly blare of Gothic trumpets.

For Christians caught in the siege, the blast of trumpets, when it came, would seem to herald the Day of Judgement. For others, steeped in Rome's past pagan glory, the trumpets would signal shame, that such a mighty city should be taken – and by barbarians. But for all then, and for us today, the Gothic trumpets sounded a turning point: the climax of an era – of long years of adaptation, progress and failure – and the prelude to a new world order.

This book will seek to find out how it all came about. Taking as its starting point Rome – a city of infinite symbolism built on intricate human contradictions – it will look at how events were sparked and shaped, both by the momentum of mass movements of distant tribes migrating across continents, and by the sometimes impulsive decisions of a few powerful individuals.

To enable us fully to appreciate the drama of AD 410, we shall first review the political and religious transformations that occurred in the preceding centuries. The political transformations, while successfully shoring up the Roman world from threats, both internal and external, had in some ways contributed to its weakness. The religious transformations, while paving the way for a new world order, had left Rome divided and caused agonies of soul-searching by pagans and Christians alike.

We shall trace the modernization of the empire's unwieldy administration by the soldier-emperor Diocletian, who regimented its civil service and compartmentalized its trades while still trusting passionately in the ability of pagan ritual to underpin Roman society. We shall see how it fell to one of his successors, Constantine, to instigate the transformative process of converting that society to Christianity. We shall consider how, in the face of border raids and growing bureaucracy, the empire was divided east and west, with the resultant rivalries between the two creating tensions of their own, while wider threats were subsumed by self-interest. And we shall explore the character and plight of the barbarians, and the ever-spiralling threats of their incursions.

As we move in closer to the sack of Rome, key players will emerge into ever-sharper focus. It is an extraordinary cast of characters, many driven by a lust for power, some ruthless, others hopelessly adrift, each with a part to play in the unfolding drama. We shall meet men like Stilicho, the half-barbarian general of Rome and, for many years, the acting emperor, who might yet have saved the empire, had he not misplayed his hand. And Alaric, the Gothic king, himself a Roman general, who more than anything wanted to find a homeland for his people; and whose mix of diplomacy and terror tactics might just have worked, had he not trusted too much in Rome's decency, and had not a series of bad timings ruined everything. We shall encounter extraordinary women, too, like the *femme fatale*, Galla Placidia, just eighteen years old when Rome was sacked, whose power and beauty would make her, by turns, a Gothic queen, a Roman empress and the effective ruler of the western Roman world.

Leading (sometimes misleading) us through it all, informing us (at times deliberately feeding us false information), is a loose-knit group of contemporary thinkers and chroniclers, who, while not actively involved in the story, have all played their part in shaping it.

There are the staunch pagan historians, like the Greek sophist Eunapius or his compatriot, the civil servant Count Zosimus. Both try hard in the pages of their histories to keep alive a spirit of historical enquiry, stretching back a thousand years to the writings of Herodotus and Thucydides, as they strive to record a human struggle played out against an epic backdrop of omens, dreams and portents of the gods' displeasure.

And there are the Christians, too: in Jerusalem, the tetchy St Jerome, hunched over his translation of the Bible, gathering news, listening to gossip, penning letters to survivors of the sack of Rome. Meanwhile, agonizing on the shores of Africa, the astute St Augustine mapped out a way to explain just how God could have allowed the newly Christianized Rome to be desecrated when, as a pagan city, it had survived intact for 800 years. Augustine's disciple, the Spanish presbyter Orosius, went on to provide a masterpiece of spin, downplaying the brutality of the God-fearing Goths while emphasizing isolated acts of Christian clemency. For all these Christian writers, history served to illustrate God's plan played out on earth. For them, what they perceived as religious truths took precedence over the inconveniences of historical fact. Yet even in their writings, we can still catch glimpses of what really happened, when for a moment they drop their guard and lift the veil to reveal the true extent of rape and slaughter on the streets of Rome.

These contemporary chroniclers, both pagan and Christian, serve as our main sources. We hear their stories in their own voices. But we are informed, too, by modern works of scholarship and archaeology; and recent interpretations and discoveries have all played a part in shaping our narrative. But *AD 410: The Year That Shook Rome* is not a work of archaeology. Nor does it attempt to explain *why* Rome fell. Rather, insofar as evidence allows, it tells the story of *how* it fell, revealing the people and events, the decisions and actions behind the siege and sack of the city.

Readers might draw parallels between some events in the late Roman world and others being played out in our world today. We have deliberately tried not to do so. History does not repeat itself, and finding patterns in the past can be misleading. And yet how people behave in times of extreme stress, in the face of make-or-break crises, has not changed so very much in the past 1,600 years. If the story of this book holds any message for us today, it is perhaps to do with what it is to be human in a time of pressure and perplexing change.

But there is another major player in our drama – one that, although it has a character and personality of its own, is not a human player. It is the city of Rome itself. And it is with Rome that our story begins.

# CHAPTER 1

# *Rome, eternal city*

*Listen to me, Rome, most lovely queen of all your world, most welcome in the star-filled heavens! Listen, nurse of men, and mother of the gods! Thanks to your temples we are close to heaven!*
(Rutilius, *On his Voyage Home to Gaul* 47–50)

Brass *sestertius*, struck at Rome in c.79–81, showing the Colosseum (see also *fig.* 1.2).

Rome, early evening, 23 August AD 410... a city under siege, brought to her knees by years of slow attrition. Exhausted by starvation and drained by false hopes, its people know that they have been abandoned, that their emperor, Honorius, has washed his hands of them.

Yet it had been not so long before that he had tried to woo them, holding out the promise that their city would again become the centre of the prosperous empire it once had been. Now, on that late August evening of 410, some must have looked back wistfully to the day six years before, when they had packed the streets to see the emperor Honorius, a mere nineteen years old, ride into Rome in triumph. His general, the wiry, grey-haired Stilicho, had conquered the barbarian chief, Alaric, and driven his hordes away from Italy. It was a time to celebrate. It was a time for Rome to dazzle.

And dazzle it did. Among Honorius' retinue, the court poet, Claudian, a Greek from Alexandria in Egypt, was skilled in the arts of flattery and spin. Although rich in exaggeration, his verses do reflect some truth. As he describes Honorius' entry into Rome, Claudian paints a glittering picture of the city and its effects on visitors.

No other city, Claudian enthuses, was more suitable as a home for emperors – it was the one place where majesty could best display itself and experience the dizzying grandeur of power. At Rome's heart, the imperial palace towered above the Forum, ringed round by countless temples and protected by innumerable gods (*fig.* 1.1). Chief among them was the Temple of Jupiter the Thunderer, with statues of giants suspended from the rock face. Below, he saw buildings with doors of sculpted bronze, 'cloud-capped' statues, and the Rostra adorned with bronze ship prows, clamped onto massive columns. Yet more temples rose from 'beetling crags' – the works of nature enhanced by the art of man – where countless arches glittered with the spoils of war. Claudian declared himself blinded by the blaze of metal, and dazzled by the sheer amount of gold.[1]

If Claudian had offered the only eyewitness account of Rome's magnificence, he might be suspected of exaggeration. But almost fifty years earlier, the much more sober writer Ammianus Marcellinus, himself a general from Syria, had been equally enthusiastic about Rome, when he accompanied the tough war-hardened emperor Constantius II on his first and only visit to the city. Based in the eastern part of the Roman Empire, Constantius had spent much of his reign in Antioch (modern Antakya in southern Turkey), a rich and powerful city. But the

**1.1** View of the Roman Forum from the Capitoline Hill: '[The emperor] went to the Rostra and looked with amazement at the Forum, that sublime monument of pristine power.' (Ammianus Marcellinus, 16.10, writing about Constantius II's visit to Rome in 357)

emperor's state entry into Rome on 28 April 357 was an event that would remain in the minds of everyone who saw it. For Constantius entered in style:

> To the right and left before him the standards filed by in line, while he alone sat in a golden carriage, dazzling and sparkling with precious stones, which shimmered and danced with light.
>
> Behind the many other divisions, he rode, surrounded by dragon-standards woven out of purple cloth and fastened to the tops of gold and jewelled spears. As the breeze blew through the gaping mouths of the dragon standards, they seemed to hiss as if roused to anger, and their long tails snaked behind them in the wind.
>
> Next came a double file of infantry in shining armour, their shields and crested helmets glittering in the sunlight. They were accompanied at intervals by cavalry in full armour, wearing masks and breastplates, and encased in iron plate and mail, so that they could have been mistaken for statues rather than living men.[2]

But it was not only the Roman Senate and people who were impressed. Exploring the city for himself, Constantius was awe-struck. Like an enthusiastic tour guide, Ammianus lists the landmarks as he saw them: the Temple of Jupiter ('surpassing in beauty any other sanctuary as much as gods surpass men'), the public baths ('as large as provinces'), the massive bulk of the Colosseum (*fig.* 1.2) ('so tall the human eye can scarcely see its top'), the Pantheon ('domed and circular, the size of a city-district'); platforms crowded with the statues of former emperors, the Temple of Rome, the Forum of Peace, the Theatre of Pompey, the Odeum, the Stadium, and ('the crowning glory') the Forum of Trajan ('which takes away even the breath of the gods').

It was a city that could trace its history back well over a thousand years; the calendar used throughout the empire dated each year '*ab urbe condita*', from the founding of Rome in 753 BC.

Although by the end of the third century AD, the Roman Empire had been divided into two halves – the eastern and western empires – Rome remained the keeper of the empire's soul. For most of Rome's history, the imperial soul was symbolized by the flame burning in the Temple of Vesta, deep in the heart of the Roman Forum. But in 391, when Christianity became the official religion of Rome, the pagan fire of Vesta had been extinguished on the orders of Honorius' father, Theodosius I.

**1.2** This brass *sestertius* of Titus (r. 79–81) depicts the Colosseum, which was opened in his reign. The largest amphitheatre in the Roman Empire, it could hold between 50,000 and 75,000 spectators. For many, the Colosseum symbolizes Rome's eternity.

By now the effect of Christianity could be felt everywhere in Rome, but it was yet to change the landscape significantly. True, a concerted building programme in the late fourth century had resulted in a flurry of great basilicas, which housed the shrines of saintly relics, like St Peter's in the Vatican and St Paul's outside the city walls. But the ancient temples, some dating back many centuries to the emperors Hadrian and Augustus and beyond, still stood, even though many were already falling into disrepair, now that public money had been diverted from their upkeep.[3] It is clear from the accounts of Claudian and Ammianus that many of these temples were still admired for their size and architecture – museum pieces in a new age.

In many respects, the fate of the temples might be perceived as mirroring that of Rome itself: a city in danger of ossifying, of becoming a centre for pageant, sightseeing and little else. For more than a hundred years now, Rome had no longer been the focus of imperial power. Instead, power resided with the emperor who, with his courtiers and much of the imperial civil service, regularly progressed across a network of cities like Trier, Milan and Ravenna (which Honorius had made his capital in 402, and where he stayed throughout 410). Wherever the court resided became for a while the current seat of empire. Even the treasury was transported in heavily laden wagons under military guard.

Despite the shift in power, Rome was far from being powerless. Its Senate was by no means simply an anachronistic throwback to the long-gone days of the Republic (509–27 BC), when the Roman world was governed by an aristocratic elite. It still wielded considerable power, not only because its members were, as individuals, some of the richest and most influential in the western empire, but because – both constitutionally and in popular perception – the Senate still had to ratify decisions of state. In recent years, the authority of the Senate had grown, as it exercised its power successfully in a series of bold moves that directly challenged both eastern and western emperors.

Moreover, in what was now an officially Christian world, many of the ancient senatorial families remained resolutely pagan, paying lip service to the new religion while privately worshipping their ancient gods. Although relatively young, the emperor Honorius was wise to the pagan sympathies of the Senate: as part of his entry ceremony in 404, he paused by the Tiber to pour a libation in honour of the ancient river god[4] – no mere act of meaningless superstition, but, rather, a deeply political gesture. In a city where much of the Senate remained obstinately pagan, an emperor needed to do all he could to make a show of public solidarity with his executive.

Meanwhile, the pagan custom of reading horoscopes remained as popular as ever; some devotees even refused to go out to dinner without consulting the stars, the planets or the moon. So to Christians and pagans alike, Rome remained the Holy City, the Eternal City, Capital of the World. The number of poems and speeches written in her honour had never before been rivalled.

And the richest Romans had much to honour her for. They lived in stratospheric luxury, their lives made ever more opulent with gems from India, spices from the Near East and silks from China. Praising the generosity of Honorius' general, Stilicho, Claudian sketches a vivid picture of the wealth of Rome:

> If fire had melted the huge weight of Stilicho's gift of silver, as if it were some base and worthless metal, then it would surely have turned into vast silver lakes and rivers.[5]

Although used to spending much of their time, especially during the unbearably sticky summers, in the coolth of their country villas, the ruling rich also enjoyed city houses that were spacious and ornate – palaces in miniature or in reality.

In his great history, *The Decline and Fall of the Roman Empire* (1776), Edward Gibbon makes much of Rome's supposed decadence – a decadence to which he attributes much of the empire's problems. He quotes Ammianus, who clearly did not greatly enjoy his visit to the city:

> Modern nobles measure their rank and consequence according to the loftiness of their chariots, and the weighty magnificence of their dress. Their long robes of silk and purple float in the wind; and as they are agitated, by art or accident, they occasionally discover the under garments, the rich tunics, embroidered with figures of various animals. ... If at any time, but more especially on a hot day, they have the courage to sail in their painted galleys from the Lucrine Lake to their elegant villas on the seacoast of Puteoli and Caieta, they compare their own expeditions to the marches of Caesar and Alexander. Yet should a fly presume to settle on the silken folds of their gilded umbrellas, should a sunbeam penetrate through some unguarded and imperceptible chink, they deplore their intolerable hardships...[6]

Subtly enhancing Ammianus' litany of complaints, Gibbon goes on to lament a trend towards anti-intellectualism:

> The acquisition of knowledge seldom engages the curiosity of nobles, who abhor the fatigue and disdain the advantages of study. ... The libraries, which they have inherited from their fathers, are secluded, like dreary sepulchres, from the light of day. But the costly instruments of the theatre, flutes, enormous lyres, and hydraulic organs, are constructed for their use; and the harmony of vocal and instrumental music is incessantly

repeated in the palaces of Rome. In those palaces sound is preferred to good sense, and the care of the body to that of the mind.

It all makes for good reading and much fun, but almost certainly does not reflect anything like the whole truth. While there was indeed luxury and 'bling', there is ample proof of more austere and challenging intellectual and spiritual pursuits as well: both classical literature, which was enjoying something of a renaissance, and Christian theology were being widely read by the rich. Although there were rich families like the Anicii, whose palace marbles 'were used as a proverbial expression of opulence and splendour',[7] it was an age of social flux, when Christianity influenced many to give their wealth away to the Church. It was often women who gave most away. One of them, Paula, once owned the entire Greek city of Nicopolis, but, inspired by her newfound faith in Christ, gave much of it to the Church. Another, Melania, also gave much of her fortune to the poor; and when she found that her house in Rome was so expensive that no one could afford to buy it, she simply donated it to the Church.

Then there was Marcella. Now in her eighty-fifth year, in 410, she was physically frail but feisty, and still showing traces of the great beauty for which she had once been renowned. She had been born into a wealthy senatorial family who owned a sprawling palace on the Aventine Hill. Many years before, after her husband's early death, Marcella had declared celibacy, dedicated her life to God, given away most of her wealth and turned her palace into a refuge for other women wishing to pursue the religious life. In effect, she founded a convent, the first monastic institution of its kind in Church history. Now, in her old age, Marcella was preparing peacefully to pass on her mantle to her favourite student, Principia, whom St Jerome would call the 'Virgin of Christ'.[8] But the events that erupted in late August 410 would have a devastating impact on Marcella and Principia, and turn all their plans to ashes…

But the almost incredible wealth once enjoyed by women like Marcella represented only one end of the scale. In a society where there was virtually no middle class, the gulf between rich and poor was enormous. Rome was by far the largest city in the world. At its height, its population was close to a million. Although by 410 the number of city dwellers was falling, there may still have been as many as 800,000. And it is salutary to reflect that – at a time when few adults could expect to live beyond the age of thirty-five or forty, and average life expectancy was just over fifteen years – the age of slightly over half the city's population was probably under twenty.[9] Its people were drawn to the city from every part of the empire, making Rome, in turn, a microcosm of the empire, a melting pot of cultures and languages, superstitions and beliefs.

Most of Rome's inhabitants lived in squalor, crowded into multi-occupancy tenements, up to six storeys high, unsafe, unsanitary, unchanged since the days of the Roman poet Juvenal, who had satirized the city's ramshackle housing two and a half centuries earlier:

> We live in a city propped up (mostly) on shaky scaffolding; oh yes!, this is how our slum landlords stop their slippages, and, as they plaster over cracks from ancient subsidence, they bid us sleep on soundly in their tottering ruins. It's better to live somewhere where there are no fires, no terrors, no alarums in the night.[10]

The conditions in and around these overcrowded tenements were almost unimaginably awful. Cramped and noisy, infested by cockroaches and rats, they were bitterly cold in winter and stifling in summer (*fig.* 1.3). Running water, where it existed, was piped only to the ground floors, where users of the communal latrines may have cleaned themselves with shared re-usable sponges. Tenants who preferred not to patronize the latrines used chamber pots instead, which were then emptied out of upper-floor windows, turning the surrounding streets and alleyways into little more than open sewers.

**1.3** The best-preserved Roman tenement houses survive at Ostia, the port of Rome. Built in the early 2nd century, this type of building housed the urban poor: 'Most sick people who live here die through lack of sleep…' (Juvenal, *Satire* III.232–5)

Those who wished to escape from domestic filth and squalor could, of course, visit the public baths. There were eleven large public bath complexes and 926 smaller baths in Rome, and bathing was clearly part of the ordinary citizen's routine. However, with doctors heartily recommending the benefits of bathing, the sick would regularly share facilities with the healthy, so that in the steam-rooms and pools, whose water was only periodically changed, bacteria could breed and disease spread almost unchecked. As a result, malaria, tuberculosis, typhoid fever and gastroenteritis ran rife.

At least most drinking water was reasonably fresh. Eleven aqueducts marched across the plains into the city to join eight other channels pouring water constantly, not only into the palaces, but also into 250 public water tanks and 1,200 fountains, which in the stifling heat of August 410 would have afforded some slight respite.

To try to preserve public health through diet, there had been for many centuries free handouts of food, and a considerable part of the imperial budget in the west was spent in making sure that the people of Rome had enough to eat. Bread, oil and salted pork were distributed free to any who could produce a means-tested ticket showing that they were living below what even the Roman government considered to be the poverty level (estimated at 30% of the population), while the price of wine was heavily subsidized.

The organization required to ensure that such vital supplies reached Rome operated on an international scale. For hundreds of years, much of Rome's foreign policy had been geared to ensuring the possession of wide tracts of land, which could be cultivated to feed the city. As Rome would quite literally shut down without these essential imports, their transport, storage and distribution had to run with constant efficiency. Grain and oil were transported from the hinterlands to the wharves of North Africa, Sicily or Spain, then loaded onto cargo ships by gangs of stevedores. When the produce reached Portus,[11] Rome's custom-built sea-port with a massive hexagonal harbour (*fig. 1.4*), the goods were unloaded, checked and temporarily stored before being transferred to barges, then towed by oxen up the Tiber, past the naval dockyards to the granaries and warehouses of Rome. From here, the grain was taken to mills, some powered by water from the aqueduct on the Janiculum Hill; others floating on rafts moored on the Tiber. After being ground in the mills, flour finally arrived at the complexes of state bakeries, where it was turned into bread. Meanwhile, countless empty olive oil jars were dumped in the south of the city at a Roman rubbish tip, now known as Monte Testaccio. Rising 40 m high and 1 km wide, the ancient waste dump contains the remains of almost twenty-five million broken amphorae.

Despite such efficiency, life in major cities like Rome, Alexandria and Constantinople was always precarious. The sheer power of numbers, possessed by the urban poor, would be a force to be reckoned with should the supply of food or wine ever fail. Food riots were far from uncommon.

1.4 Coin of Nero (r. 54–68), struck at Rome, showing the harbour at Portus, north of Ostia. The hexagonal basin enclosed an area of 39 hectares and was linked by canal to the River Tiber.

Ammianus describes protests in Rome a couple of generations earlier over a shortage of wine. 'For', he observes wearily, 'the common people, desperate for its unrestricted consumption, are often moved to stage violent disturbances.'[12]

The relationship between the Roman poor and their super-rich rulers was always under potential strain. The urbane Ammianus, himself from Antioch in Syria, was singularly unimpressed by the Roman underclass (as, indeed, he was by their 'betters'). Although his description of the poor is probably exaggerated, it does make worthwhile reading and helps us build up a picture of life in Rome in the late fourth century:

**1.5** A gladiator with trident and sword at the base of a glass drinking vessel, probably found in the catacombs, Rome, dating from the late 4th century. The inscription reads: 'You have won well in Stratoniceia [in Turkey]; go to Aurelia [northern Italy]; drink that you may live.'

Of the masses – those from the lowest and most impoverished classes – some spend the night in bars and wine-shops, while quite a few skulk in the shadows of theatre awnings … or quarrel violently over games of dice, making a revolting, thunderous noise as they hawk in their breath through flaring nostrils. Or – and this is the most popular of any of their pursuits – from sunrise to sunset, rain or shine, they stand around, gawping and scrutinizing in the most minute detail the pros and cons of charioteers and horses. It is absolutely incredible to see the countless throngs of commoners, their minds filled with a passion all their own, hanging on the result of some chariot race. These, and similar things, mean that nothing significant or serious can be achieved in Rome.[13]

Juvenal had a famous recipe for preserving order in Rome: bread and circuses. Ammianus' wry account of chariot-racing goes to the heart of the second ingredient – entertainment and spectacle were key elements in Roman life. In 410, the Colosseum was still very much in service: although gladiatorial combats had not been held for six years (not since 404, when a monk had been ripped to shreds as he tried to stop the games), wild animal hunts would continue for more than a century (*fig.* 1.5).

Meanwhile, a quarter of a million people regularly flocked to the Circus Maximus, not only to watch their favourite chariot teams compete, but also to see their rulers (*fig.* 1.6). For, nestling between the Palatine and the Tiber, the circus was perfectly placed: with a discreet entrance to the imperial box from the palace complex, it offered the ideal venue where the people could most conveniently commune with their rulers. It was, more than anywhere else, a place where the three elements of Roman society, emperor, Senate and people, could meet.

As such, it was the stage for great state occasions, spectacles and carefully choreographed displays of Roman power. After his entry into Rome in 404, Honorius took his seat in the imperial box beside his general, the powerful Stilicho. With them, we might imagine, were Honorius' half-sister, fourteen-year-old Galla Placidia; and Stilicho's son, the young Eucherius, to whom she was betrothed. Claudian describes the scene:

**1.6** Copper alloy *Contorniate*, 4th century. Possibly used as a gaming counter, the reverse shows the Circus Maximus with chariots and wild animals (see also *fig.* 9.5). 'Again and again our ears ring in amazement with the roar of the Circus.' (Rutilius Namatianus, *A Voyage Home to Gaul*, 201)

The roar of the adoring multitude… rises up like thunder from the hollow bowl of the arena, reverberating round the seven hills to echo back as one the name 'Honorius'.
Here in the circus military displays, too, are staged. Here we can often see armed squadrons fan out and advance, wheel round and fall back again in perfect order and tight discipline; a fine display, a thrilling artifice of war. The master sounds the order with his whip. In perfect unison, the massed ranks perform their new manoeuvres, clashing their shields against their sides or shaking them above their heads; the round shields resonate low, the swords ring sharp and clear, creating a symphony, a rhythmic beating, with swords and shields in harmony.

As one, the phalanx kneels. A sea of helmets bows in salute before you, our leader. Then the troops split and spiral, running out in well-rehearsed formation … they wheel apart again and coil back in tight formation. So Janus cages conflict behind closed doors[14] which will stay shut forever; and now, with the happy masquerade of battle done, Janus bestows on Peace the prizes of prosperity – hard won from War.[15]

**1.7** Gold medallion of Honorius (r. 395–423), with a suspension loop, c.404. The reverse shows Roma enthroned, with the inscription, 'The glory of the Romans'. It was probably struck in celebration of Honorius' visit to Rome in 404.

This impressive military display, staged in part to celebrate Stilicho's victory over the Goths the year before, may have represented the last flowering of popular confidence in Rome. Fearing for the city's safety, Honorius had already enlarged and strengthened its walls in a major three-year project, doubling their height to 12 m and extending them south of the river to include the district now called Trastevere. It was partly to inspect the new walls that Honorius had visited Rome in 404; and partly, too, to reassure its citizens, through shows of military might, that they were in safe hands (*fig.* 1.7).

Yet now, on 23 August 410, the memory of that immaculately stage-managed but ultimately empty display six years earlier, with its carefully rehearsed manoeuvres and make-believe battles celebrating a far-off victory over Alaric the Goth, must have been in the minds of not a few.

For now, on this oppressively hot and sticky night, as the stench from the Tiber crept damp and foetid through the city air, Alaric with his wagons and warriors was encamped where the sun was setting low beyond the western walls of Rome. In just a few hours, the fate of the Eternal City – the city of Romulus and Caesar, the Sacred City, intact, unbreached for 800 years, the 'first among cities, home of the gods, golden Rome'[16]– would be reversed. How, they must have wondered, had it come to this?

Prologue

PART 1

*A house divided*

# CHAPTER 2

# *A new world order*

*May Jupiter in heaven forbid the barbarians ever to outrage — even by so much as looking at them — Numa's shrine or Romulus' temple; and let them not uncover the hidden secrets of our great empire.*
(Claudian, *Gothic War* 100–3)

The Goths massing at the city gates on that late August day in AD 410 were not the first barbarians the Roman world had seen; and they were far from being the most barbaric.

Today we tend to use the word 'barbarian' to mean someone uncivilized and brutish, but its derivation contains no such connotations. It was the Greeks who first coined the word *barbaros*, as a useful onomatopoeia for the sheep-like baa-ing of anyone who did not speak 'civilized' Greek. The *barbaroi* lived outside the Greek-speaking world, in cultures such as Persia or Egypt, which had, paradoxically, reached a far higher degree of civilization than most of the mud-brick villages of mainland Greece. For the Greeks, of course, the *barbaroi* also included the newly emerging civilization of Rome.

Naturally, a word so redolent of linguistic and cultural exclusivity began to take on prejudicial overtones. For Greeks, who believed in the superiority not only of their political ideals of freedom and democracy but also of their physical and intellectual prowess, *barbaroi* were demonstrably inferior. The pejorative connotations of the word had been born (*fig.* 2.1).

When the Romans overran Greece in the second century BC, sacking Corinth, one of antiquity's great centres of civilization, they returned not only with looted artworks, but with looted language and ideas, among them the concept of the barbarian.

The idea would be adopted but altered by the Romans to mean anyone living outside Rome's sphere of rule, the antithesis of the urbane Roman living under the Republic and, subsequently, under the expanding empire.

As the legions conquered ever-greater swathes of Europe, so the number of barbarians being assimilated under Rome's rule increased. Traces of this assimilation still survive in cities like Bath, where the healing springs of the 'barbarian' goddess Sulis were adorned with marble and became the centre of a fashionable Roman spa.

2.1 Marble statue of a barbarian, probably clutching at the skirt of Victory, from the Palace of Trajan at Ramleh in Egypt, c.160–70. 'Remember, Roman: rule all people with your power; impose the way of peace (this is your special skill); spare the humble and defeat the proud.' (Virgil, *Aeneid* vi, 851ff.)

But as the empire grew, so, of course, did its boundaries; and, from the early years of the first century AD, bloody border conflicts with barbarians took up much of the army's attention. In the south and west, the Roman world was protected by the natural barriers of desert and sea, but to the north and east lay volatile tribes and powerful empires, all looking for new territories, all increasing the pressure on Rome's borders.

By the mid-third century AD, border pressure became increasingly unmanageable. In Europe, coordinated attacks across the Danube and the Rhine led to vast tracts of empire in modern Germany and Romania being lost forever; while in the Near East, the Roman emperor Valerian was led away to ignominious slavery when Mesopotamia fell to the Persians in 260.

It was a desperate situation, and one compounded by a lack of any real stability in the empire, where a paltry pageant of usurping emperors – many of them career soldiers raised to the purple[17] by a disgruntled army – periodically seized power only to lose it again a few years later. In the period immediately following Valerian's disaster in the east, these soldier-emperors did succeed in staunching the haemorrhaging borders, but there was little doubt that the empire was becoming weaker and more unwieldy.

Enter Diocletian, the burly, brutal, yet brilliant cavalry commander, hailed Emperor of Rome to the full-throated acclamation of the massed ranks of his troops, his sword still dripping with his rival's blood (*fig. 2.2*). Ruthlessly determined, he seized the stumbling empire by the scruff of its neck and, like the tough drill sergeant he may once have been, set about reshaping and reforming it until it was, in his mind, 'fit for purpose'. The result was a radical new system of government, whose implications would have a profound effect not only on the Roman empire of his day, but on the subsequent history of the medieval and early modern world.

Diocletian assumed power in 284 and began work immediately. Being a military man, some of his first reforms involved the army. Not only did he apparently increase its size, on paper at least,[18] to around 600,000; but also, being aware of the importance of the edges of the empire, he expended much of his energy on strengthening the frontiers and their garrisons with specialist border troops. To support these troops, a highly mobile army of crack regiments was later formed, both infantry and cavalry, which could be rapidly deployed to any trouble spots throughout the empire.

**2.2** Gold medallion of Diocletian, struck in 294 at Nicomedia (at that time his capital in the eastern empire). The reverse shows Jupiter the Protector, Diocletian's 'guardian companion'.

One of the results of his reforms was to deprive the once formidable provincial governors of the military power-bases from which they had plotted their *coups d'état*. Instead, they became mere administrators, cogs in the wheel of an imperial civil service; and, even here, their potential to seize power was diminished by Diocletian's radical redrawing of provincial boundaries and downscaling of the provinces, in both size and importance. Inadvertently, however, his measures created a situation in which the generals of the field army, powerful men with the support of great bodies of troops, could in time rise to unchallengeable military and political power. Ironically, many of these field generals (like Stilicho and Alaric) would be barbarians.

That Diocletian felt secure enough, after

Part 1 A house divided

twenty-one years of rule, to retire to his coastal villa at Split (in modern Croatia) shows that, for him at least, his military reforms had succeeded. But there was a major downside, and one not confined to the army.

By parcelling out power and arranging it into a network of hierarchies, each answerable ultimately to the imperial court, Diocletian had sown the seeds of a bureaucracy that would grow increasingly convoluted and arcane. In time, one of the two centres of imperial power – the eastern, Byzantine Empire – would become so labyrinthine and opaque in its style of government that the word 'byzantine' came to mean 'convoluted' and 'treacherous'.

For in Diocletian's raft of big ideas, the biggest of them all was to divide the empire into two, east and west, ruled by two emperors, with two parallel administrations. Trier, Milan and Rome became the centres of the western empire; meanwhile, the eastern court migrated between Thessalonica in Greece, Antioch in the Levant and Nicomedia on the shores of the Sea of Marmara, all so much closer to potential flashpoints at the borders with barbarians.

Each of the two emperors, or *Augusti*, had his own deputy or *Caesar*, who was also the emperor's designated successor *(fig.* 2.3*)*. The thinking behind Diocletian's system, the so-called Tetrarchy (rule of four), is clear. By removing the ultimate power from one man and sharing it between four (two *Augusti* and two *Caesares*), it would, thought Diocletian, be impossible for usurpers to rise up and overthrow the government. The empire would be stable, the future secure.

But a stable empire would only be feasible if both halves could continue to work in harmony. Yet, as will be seen, Diocletian's momentous decisions generated profound and long-lasting tensions, not only between those for and against a unified empire, but more crucially between the eastern and western empires, both increasingly threatened by external constraints and internal collapse.

**2.3** Porphyry statue of the tetrarchs, c.300, on the corner of St Mark's Basilica, Venice: 'Diocletian divided the world into four parts and appointed three men to share its rule with him.' (Lactantius, *On the Deaths of the Persecutors* 7)

The capital city of each empire had its own imperial court with its own painstakingly gradated regiments of civil servants, organized (how else?) like a bureaucratic army. It happens that an official document, the *Notitia Dignitatum*, survives from the turn of the fifth century, listing the offices of state in the four praetorian prefectures of Gaul, Italy, Illyricum and the East. It reveals a pen pusher's paradise of esoteric functionaries, ranging from diplomatic mandarins to domestic flunkies. The list includes everyone from the prefects themselves to the Accountant of Private Property in Britain, the Tribune of the Swine Market in Rome and the separate Provosts and Superintendents of the Sacred Bedchamber. It also includes illustrations of the elaborate coats-of-arms that became a feature of the empire's civil offices.

One of the effects of Diocletian's new bureaucracy was to emasculate its officials – in many cases quite literally, as the top jobs in the growing civil service began increasingly to be filled by eunuchs, who were, of course, in no position to have any dynastic ambitions of their own. Over the years, his bureaucracy gave rise to strangulating red tape and abuse of power; but, occasionally, amid the stultifying lists of provincial administrators, we catch glimpses of another side of public life, as in the writings of John the Lydian. A disgruntled civil servant, piqued at being passed over for preferment, he published his unexpurgated memoirs in the middle of the sixth century. In their pages lurk such colourful characters as John the Cappadocian:

> Even as naked pleasure-girls were fondling him, other prostitutes would lead him on his way with rampant kisses, leaving him no option but to have sex there and then. Then, when he was spent, he would snatch sweet canapés and drinks from the outstretched hands of other catamites. So many and so sweet and frothy were the drinks, that, when he could no longer keep them down, he just vomited, like a mighty river that has breached its banks, flooding the whole house – and no small danger to his hangers-on, who would slide and skid about on the glistening mosaic floors.[19]

John the Lydian was writing nearly 300 years after Diocletian's reforms. His gossip shows how far things had degenerated from what had been envisaged. But even in Diocletian's day, the trend was being set as the bureaucracy grew in size, its staff decked out in military-style uniforms; its elite core surrounding an increasingly remote emperor; its protocol becoming ever more ritualistic. Opportunities for corruption grew. Venality and self-interest became the norm. Yet it was thanks mainly to Diocletian's new civil service that the empire could weather weak or infant emperors.

If the army and the civil service were growing in size, elsewhere the empire was experiencing a worrying reduction in manpower. Since the late second century, the population seems to have declined steadily, caused in part by the barbarian invasions and civil wars, which affected not only the army, but also the wider countryside and towns. Numbers had been reduced, too, by the plagues that had swept through the Roman world in the second and third centuries. Yet, even as the population declined, its need to fund an expanding army and bureaucracy grew, inevitably causing social tension.

A general feeling of instability, linked to a breakdown of law and order in the late third century, seems to have led large groups of peasant-farmers to flee their lands and join renegade bands of dispossessed outlaws, the so-called *bagaudae*. In the years immediately preceding Diocletian's accession, a succession of successful campaigns had been waged against the *bagaudae*; and their lands had been confiscated and resettled. But how and by whom their lands were resettled would have a quite unforeseen impact on the entire Roman Empire for centuries to come. For, often the land was parcelled out not to the indigenous peoples but to incomers, to barbarians from Germany, as a reward for their service as mercenaries, and as a guarantee that their children would provide recruits for the imperial army (*fig.* 2.4). Increasingly, if implicitly, the

**2.4** Copper alloy belt buckle, late 4th or early 5th centuries, found in Kent. Such buckles were used by Roman soldiers, federate troops fighting for Rome, and even soldiers in Britain after the collapse of Britannia in 407/11.

Roman world was relying more and more on immigrant labour. Civilization was being kept alive by the barbarians.

Having inherited the problem, Diocletian tackled it by legislating to prevent farmers from leaving their land. At the same time, he introduced a new system of taxation, worked out on a per capita basis, by which farms must provide produce directly to central authorities. The result of his measures was a gradual diminution in the number of independent farmers as smallholders, who became increasingly subsumed into larger estates, were forced to exchange freedom for security. It was the beginning of serfdom, a prelude to feudalism, which would so characterize life in the Middle Ages. How immediately successful it was is less clear. As food production continued to decline, vast areas of Italy and Africa became known as the *agri deserti* (the deserted fields). Yet the power of rich landowners grew as their estates spread ever outwards, while those who had worked the land made increasingly desperate attempts to flee it (*fig. 2.5*).

But even if they made it to the cities, the displaced farmers found that opportunities for work were shrinking, and that there were many trades from which they were completely debarred. This, too, was down to Diocletian, whose legislation included trade-fixing measures to ensure that certain skills were kept in the family. So, in those sectors essential for the smooth running of the empire, sons were now obliged to take up the same profession as their fathers, whether in the military, in armament factories, in transport or on the land. The opportunity for social mobility had been frozen. Personal liberties had been curtailed. The Roman citizen, who for centuries had enjoyed a proud and enviable freedom, had become a powerless subject of the state as his masters scrabbled to shore up the shaky military and economic infrastructures of empire.

It was not only the poorer classes who bore the brunt of Diocletian's legislation. Despite his attempts at economic reform – fixing prices and stabilizing the currency – it was still a time of high inflation, during which town councillors (another profession in which sons were obliged to follow their fathers into office) were held responsible for ensuring that strict targets were met for tax revenues. Any shortfalls had to be paid out of their own pockets. It was a recipe for exploitation; and, like much of Diocletian's other legislation, it contained the seeds of personal disaffection, alienation and unrest, which would later spill over into public protest:

> The situation was so bad that the inhabitants of Antioch, the great city in Syria, were unable to put up with the new taxes, which the collectors invented every day. So they rioted and pulled down the statues of the emperor and his wife.[20]

Yet Diocletian believed that what would hold the system together was his newly powerful behemoth of bureaucratic government grafted to the unyielding strength of the ancient state religion. In this he was mistaken.

Already by the late third century, Christianity had spread throughout the Roman world. Fluid in its network of associations and strong in its appeal, Christianity represented a real alternative to Diocletian's rigid new world order. The new faith drew not only the disenfranchised but all those who sought some certainty in a world that seemed to be disintegrating around them. But that was not all. Christians refused to worship the emperor. Clearly, they posed a threat. And any threat to the empire had to be dealt with.

For a time, Diocletian hoped that by simply barring Christians from holding military or public office, he could contain their influence. But his *Caesar* Galerius disagreed. He believed that more stringent measures should be taken. So in 303, according to the Church fathers,[21] the two men decided to resolve the issue by consulting the oracle of Apollo at Didyma (in modern western Turkey). But the oracle could not provide an answer – Apollo's powers, it said, were being interfered with by 'the Just on earth'.

**2.5** Bronze statuette of a plough team, 1st–3rd century, Piercebridge, Britain. The ploughman's hooded cloak was a famous British product, being mentioned in Diocletian's 'Price Edict' (301). Britain was a major source of grain for the Roman army in Germany in the 4th century.

Galerius and the court knew exactly what the oracle meant. The 'Just on earth' were the Christians. For the empire – so inexorably intertwined with its pagan gods – to survive, Christianity must be eradicated.

The persecutions that followed were widespread and systematic. Their vigour was compounded by the fact that only days after Diocletian had published his 'Edict Against the Christians' (303), ordering the destruction of churches and the burning of books, the imperial palace at Nicomedia, where the court was spending the winter, was consumed by fire. Galerius' reaction was swift. Clergy and laity alike were rounded up and executed.

But Diocletian himself, perhaps aware of the extent to which Christianity had taken hold throughout the empire, preferred a less violent solution. In an attempt to debilitate the increasingly powerful religion, Christians were banned from assembling to worship; their civic rights, including the right to defence in a court of law, were removed; their sacred texts were confiscated; and any Christian holding public office was stripped of his post. When these measures failed to have much effect, members of the clergy were arrested. As prisons throughout the empire filled to overflowing, it was announced that any who agreed to take part in pagan sacrifices would be set free. But the system was open to such abuse that finally, in the last months of his reign, Diocletian ordered that Christians be brought together in public spaces and forced to sacrifice before the gods. Any who refused would be put to death.

If Diocletian's edicts revealed anything, it was the sheer number and determination of Christians now spread throughout the empire. When he resigned from office in May 305, he might have reflected how, at the beginning of his reign, the greatest threat to stability came from outside the empire's borders. Now the greatest threat seemed to be homegrown, rooted in a belief system taking hold in every province and at every level – everywhere. He could not know that his successor in the west, Constantius I, would live for little over a year; nor that Constantius' son, Constantine I, would change the face of the Roman world for ever.

# CHAPTER 3

# *Rome baptized*

*I know for certain that I owe my whole life
and my every breath, each thought that comes
into my mind, to the Almighty God.*
(Eusebius, quoting Constantine
in his *Life of Constantine* II.29.1)

On a late July day in 306, the Roman army in Britain gathered on the north bank of the River Ouse at York to witness the funeral of a god. The Divine Constantius, emperor of the west, was dead.

The traditional imperial memorial service would have been a spectacularly theatrical event.[22] After a relatively low-key private funeral, a waxen effigy of the dead emperor was put on public display, the focus of public mourning. When the due day came, the effigy was taken to ·the funeral pyre, a towering edifice, tall as a temple and as ornate, which was adorned with statues, garlands and rich ornaments; and piled high with gifts sent from across the province and the empire. The solemn ranks of soldiers in full armour, and the cavalry – their horses brushed till their coats shone – circled the great pyre for one last time. Then the fires were lit and the whole construction caught and crackled. As the effigy began to melt, a trapdoor high up on the pyre was sprung, and from below the gathered congregation saw an eagle soaring far above the flames. The apotheosis was complete. The soul of the dead emperor had risen to the heavens to take its place beside the gods (*fig.* 3.1).

But while the eagle soared across the North York Moors, relishing its newfound freedom, events in York itself were unfolding apace. According to the rules recently laid down by Diocletian, an emperor, or *Augustus*, should be succeeded by his

Detail of the Christian Chi-Rho symbol from the Hinton St Mary villa mosaic, Dorset, mid-4th century (see also *fig.* 3.2).
.

deputy, or *Caesar*. But the army and the court in Britain wanted none of this. Instead, on the parade ground outside their great headquarters building, the Roman legions had already made their choice, acclaiming as their new emperor, their general Constantine, Constantius' eldest son.

Although in later life he liked to cut a dash, with his long hair, jewelled robes and gem-encrusted helmet, Constantine was an army man to his bones. He had been brought up in Diocletian's court in Nicomedia. After the usual education in the Latin and Greek classics, as well as in philosophy, he served with distinction in military commands on the threatened borders of the east. Constantine was present when Diocletian passed his edict persecuting the Christians,[23] an edict

**3.1** Copper alloy commemorative coin of Constantius I (r. 293–306), struck at London in 307–10. The obverse titles the dead emperor as the divine and pious Constantius. On the reverse, the inscription proclaims *memoria felix* (fond memories) with eagles on either side of an altar (see also *fig*. 5.4).

masterminded, some said, by Galerius; and, according to Christian sources, it was partly to escape Galerius' hatred that Constantine found his way to Britain and his father's court.

Now, with support for his appointment spreading throughout the western provinces, Constantine acted swiftly. In keeping with ancient practice, he sent on to Rome an announcement of his elevation – 'forced on him' by the army – along with a portrait of himself, robed in imperial purple, the portrait itself wreathed in symbolic bay leaves. Then, knowing that his rivals were unlikely meekly to accept him as their emperor, he crossed with his army into Gaul and started on the long road south to Rome.

If this was his first step on the path to sole command, he was still a long way from his goal. In October 312, Constantine faced Maxentius, his one surviving rival in the west, at the Milvian Bridge near Rome. The outcome of the ensuing battle would decide the fate of the empire, but it is the events immediately leading up to the battle that have exercised the minds of historians and theologians ever since.

All his life, Constantine had been aware of Christianity. It is likely that Hosius, bishop of Corduba, had for some time accompanied him as part of his retinue, no doubt advising the young Constantine on how the God of the Old Testament supported his people in battle.

But quite apart from the inspiring example of any one individual, Constantine must have been aware of the strength of the Church's network and the passionate fervour that Christianity excited. He may have been aware, too – especially having seen the comparative failure of Diocletian's persecutions – that the tide had turned and that, in this new empire of faceless bureaucrats, the time had come for a religion that promised personal salvation. If this desire for personal salvation could be channelled through the state, then so much the better.

Whatever his thinking, as the struggle for the western empire reached its climax, Constantine had, it seems, already resolved to put his faith in Christianity when, at prayer before the Battle of the Milvian Bridge, he had a vision, later described by the Church historian Eusebius:

> While the emperor was praying and making his fervent devotions, a remarkable vision came to him from God. If anyone else had told [the story], it might not have been so readily believed. But, as the victorious emperor himself related it, many years later, to the writer of this present work (when he was honoured to know him and enjoy his company), and since he swore the truth of it on oath, who could not believe his evidence?
>
> He said that at about midday, when the sun had already passed its highest, he saw with his own eyes, in the sky above the sun, the sign of the cross, along with the words: 'With this, be victorious'. When he saw the vision, he was struck with awe – as was his whole army, which witnessed the miracle, too.[24]

The next night, Constantine went on to tell Eusebius, Christ had appeared to him in a dream and (appealing, apparently, to the emperor's penchant for gemstones) ordered him to have a standard constructed of gold and precious jewels. Eusebius, who subsequently saw the standard, describes it as:

> a long gilded spear with a horizontal bar formed the sign of the cross. At the top was a circlet of gold and costly jewels, in the centre of which was the symbol of our Saviour's name: the first two letters of the name of Christ, the letter Rho [P] being crossed through with the letter Chi [X]. Later, the emperor would always wear these letters on his helmet. From the crossbar of the spear hung a royal banner, richly embroidered and shimmering with precious stones, all lavishly stitched with gold thread. It is impossible to describe its beauty or its effect on those who saw it. The banner was square. On its upper part, beneath the sign of the cross and immediately above the embroidered panel, it bore a half-length portrait[25] of the devout emperor with his children [*fig. 3.2*].[26]

As the banner, redolent with Christian and imperial symbolism, was paraded before them, Constantine's army bayed the *barritus*, their deep-throated war-cry, which rose to a deafening crescendo as they beat their spear shafts rhythmically against their shields. In the carnage that followed, Constantine's new Christian army routed its enemy, forcing them back into the Tiber, pursuing those who fled and cutting down any they could find (*fig. 3.3*). When the body of the defeated general Maxentius was found among the dead, Constantine had its head hacked off and paraded round the streets of Rome, then sent on spear-tip to North Africa to be displayed in Carthage as a sign to Rome's breadbasket that the regime had changed. To celebrate his victory in Rome itself, Constantine erected an arch, complete with sculptures depicting the bloody slaughter (*fig. 3.3*).

**3.2** The Hinton St Mary villa mosaic, from Dorset, mid-4th century, features a male head facing, with the Chi-Rho symbol behind. The pomegranates on either side are an ancient symbol of eternal life. The authors believe the figure to be Christ, but some think it shows Constantine I (r. 306–37).

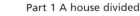

Part 1 A house divided

**3.3** Sculptural relief from the Arch of Constantine in Rome, built in 315. The scene is one of several showing the Battle of the Milvian Bridge in 312. Constantine's army drives Maxentius' troops into the Tiber. The inscription on the Arch proclaims that Constantine 'won by the inspiration of the deity [the Christian God] and greatness of mind'.

If the Christian God had helped Constantine, then Constantine, in good pagan fashion, honoured his new benefactor. One of his first acts as emperor in 313 was to issue the 'Edict of Toleration', which legitimized Christianity throughout the empire. From now on, in theory at least, Christians could no longer be persecuted for their beliefs. It was a turning point in European culture, but not all parts of the empire turned at the same speed. Although Constantine's co-emperor in the east, Licinius, rubber-stamped the edict and followed Constantine's example in leading his armies to victory under the standard of Christianity, he nonetheless continued actively to oppose Christianity in the eastern provinces, while emblazoning on his newly minted coinage the image of Jupiter the Protector.

But Licinius was not alone in his attitude or actions. For, as many as five years after the 'Edict of Toleration', the coinage issued by Constantine himself bore the image of the sun god, *Sol Invictus* (the Invincible Sun). When, in 321, he made Sunday special by decreeing that law courts and workshops should be closed on 'the venerable day of the Sun', it is questionable whether he was honouring the Christian God, the pagan *Sol*, or (in an act of typical Roman syncretism[27]) both (*fig.* 3.4).

It might appear that, in supporting Christ, Constantine was simply adding yet another deity to the pantheon of pagan gods already worshipped throughout the empire. It was a pantheon

**3.4** Gold pendant set with a coin of Constantine I, struck in 321. With hand upraised in a gesture of speech, the emperor wears the radiate crown of Sol, the Roman sun god. The six classical busts surrounding Constantine may represent Greek gods, philosophers, muses or satyrs.

that had been swollen throughout history by new imports such as Mithras, the Zoroastrian sun god from Persia, who was popular with the legions; or the Egyptian mother goddess Isis, who was often depicted in art suckling her baby Osiris, and who would become virtually indistinct from the cult of the Virgin Mary and infant Christ.[28] But Constantine's actions show clearly that his stance on Christianity was not simply another example of Roman syncretism. In his years as emperor, he issued a raft of legislation designed actively to encourage Christianity and accommodate its adherents, while gradually removing support from the traditional religion of Rome.

Some of his reforms encouraging Christianity had localized effects on other sectors of the empire. Early in his reign, for instance, he earmarked quantities of food from Africa specifically for distribution among Christian communities. Bishops were allowed to try cases in a civic dispute, if both parties agreed to the arrangement. It was also decreed that ceremonies for freeing slaves might legally be carried out in churches. Another edict outlawed the branding of convicts on the face (on the grounds that the face, having been created in the image of God, should not be disfigured). As a mark of respect to the crucified Christ, crucifixion, the traditional Roman method of executing criminals, was also banned; burning at the stake was introduced instead.

But other reforms had more lasting implications, which subtly but irrevocably undermined some of the ancient pillars of Roman stability. Some affected public life. Within the imperial court, Constantine himself forbade pagan worship, actively recruiting Christians as his courtiers, while throughout the empire Christians were excused from the burdensome task of serving on town councils (which not only encouraged the more savvy pagans to convert, but also reduced the pool of good candidates for civic office). Other reforms affected private life. Centuries-old legislation designed to increase the Roman population, which had imposed heavy penalties on childless individuals, was repealed, allowing Christians to practise celibacy – this despite a seemingly falling population and manpower in parts of the empire. Still other reforms affected both private and public life. Religious bequests were legalized, allowing fervent converts to swell the coffers of the Church, rather than leave their riches to their children or, if without offspring, to other family members.

And the Church was becoming very rich indeed. In his first years as emperor, Constantine had endowed it with vast tracts of land, rich swathes of Italy and Sicily, of Africa and the eastern provinces, all of which brought in staggering revenues to Rome's

**3.5** The church of St Sabina, built by Peter of Illyria, a priest from Dalmatia, c.422–32. Although restored on several occasions, it is still an excellent example of an early basilica. It was built on the Aventine Hill near where the Roman matriarch Marcella turned her palace into a 'convent' for Christian women.

newly founded churches (*fig. 3.5*): St John's Lateran, St Paul's Outside the Walls, St Peter's on the Vatican. With each church that sprang up, the face of Rome kept changing. It was becoming Christian.

But Rome was not to be the empire's first great Christian city. In 323, Constantine turned his forces against his erstwhile ally, Licinius, the emperor of the east; and in the next year, after a series of hard-fought battles, he defeated him. Now Constantine was supreme ruler of both east and west. To mark his victory, he decreed the building of a new city, an eastern capital, a sister of Rome in the west. It was to be built at Byzantium and christened as the city of the emperor Constantine – Constantinople (modern Istanbul) (*fig. 3.6*).

At the spiritual heart of Constantinople lay its churches – great ornate basilicas such as *Agia Eirene* (Holy Peace) and *Agia Sophia* (Holy Wisdom). Meanwhile, as Constantine kept confiscating money from the ancient pagan treasuries, and artworks from their sanctuaries, his city basked in the reflected glory of a thousand years of culture, becoming a museum of the riches of a bygone age. The gold and ivory statue of Zeus from Olympia, one of the wonders of the ancient world, is said to have been brought to the new city, where its face became the model for the face of Christ that would appear on countless frescoes in Byzantine churches. Today, the great bronze serpent monument, at the base of the so-called Tripod of Plataea,[29] looted from Apollo's shrine at Delphi, can still be seen, broken and tarnished on the *spina* (central barrier) of the Hippodrome in modern Istanbul.

But it was not only art that poured into Constantinople. Like Rome, the city needed to be fed. So, following the Roman model, Constantine provided his new citizens with free rations of wheat, imported from the empire's eastern breadbasket, Egypt. And if the people of Constantinople were treated in accordance with their counterparts in Rome, so was its Senate, set up in mirror image to the Senate in the west. But the two Senates were not equal. In a move that would have repercussions long after his death, Constantine

**3.6** Silver and gilt ornament personifying Constantinople, found on the Esquiline Hill in Rome, later 4th century (see *fig.*10.4). Constantinople bears a *patera* (dish used for sacrifices) and *cornucopiae* (horn of plenty). Three other ornaments, personifying Rome, Antioch and Alexandria, made up the set.

decreed that the Senate of Rome should be supreme. In any dispute between the cities, Constantinople must come second.

It must have truly seemed to Constantine as though through him a new heaven and a new earth had been created. But if he had hoped for harmony, it was not to be. Persecuted, the Church had managed to stay more or less united. Legitimized, it quickly fell apart.

The first cracks emerged in Africa and had their origins in the Christian persecutions themselves. At first, the trouble seemed to be little more than recriminatory bickering over who had done what and when during the last days of Diocletian's rule. Charges of collaboration and betrayal were levelled at priests accused of handing over copies of the sacred scriptures to avoid punishment.[30] A Church Council was convened and a ruling passed. Had both sides accepted the ruling, that would have been an end of it. But they did not, and so the squabble escalated.

As an example of brotherly love, it left a lot to be desired. For Constantine, it was deeply worrying. If the Church, on which his rule was founded, could not be united, what did that presage for the empire itself? He quickly penned a letter to Aelafius, the deputy praetorian prefect of Africa:

> Since I have been well informed that you, too, worship Almighty God, I shall confess to you that I think it contrary to the will of God that we should in any way ignore these quarrels and disagreements, which might incite Almighty God to act not only against the human race but against me in person, into whose care He has, by His divine will, commended the government of everything on earth – and it might make Him do something utterly unforeseen. Truly I shall be able to feel secure and able constantly to hope for great prosperity and success from the most ready beneficence of Almighty God only when I know that all peoples are glorifying God the Most Holy as they should – in the Catholic faith and in a united fellowship of worship. Amen.[31]

Constantine had already been petitioned for support by both sides in the dispute, but, wisely, he had refused to get involved. Now, though, when the losing side refused to accept the judgement of the Church Council, it was clear that he had no option. He convened an Ecumenical Council, which upheld the previous decision of the Church Council; but, once more, the losing side refused to accept its ruling. Loathe to act against Christian brothers, Constantine merely condemned them as 'impious criminals', and left their punishment to God.

If this episode had shown the emperor's weakness in the face of Church schism, it was nothing compared to what would follow. Fresh from his victory over Licinius and buoyant in his belief in a united Christian empire, Constantine rode in triumph into Nicomedia, and straight into the eye of an ecclesiastical storm. But this time the dispute was not about recrimination for betrayal under stress. This time it was doctrinal.

At the heart of the Arian Controversy lay the nature of the Trinity, or more precisely the relationship between God the Father and Christ the Son. The generally accepted view was that God, Christ and the Holy Spirit were of one and the same substance, but the Egyptian theologian Arius argued that Christ was not only independent of God, but there had been a time when he had not existed. Initial attempts to resolve the problem failed. So in 325, Constantine summoned an Ecumenical Council at Nicaea where he presided over a long and heated debate between 300 bishops from across the empire. In the end, Constantine suggested a fudge, unacceptable to Arius, and consequently accepted by Arius' opponents.

But the problem did not go away. Despite his new status as a heretic, Arius continued to attract adherents in significant numbers, adherents who were to include the future emperors Constantius II and Valens, as well as Alaric, the future sacker of Rome. For the first time since the persecution, Christianity had become sectarian, with all the tensions, hatred and potential for violence that sectarianism brings in its train.

Arius was not alone in questioning the basic tenets of Christianity or in seeking his own path to salvation. All over the empire, but especially in the east, people had been turning their backs on the conventionally organized Church for some time, retreating into the desert, renouncing the world and giving up their lives to the contemplation of God. Already in the time of the emperor Diocletian (284–305), St Antony is said to have struck out deep into the Egyptian desert as far from human communion as he could go, and when, against his will, he was joined by waves of disciples attracted by his piety, he created the first community of hermits there in 305.

In the west, too, rich men and women had begun to give up their wealth to lead austere lives in the service of Christ. There were men like Paulinus; brought up as part of a rich family in Bordeaux, he donated his wealth to the Church and to the poor before founding a monastery by the tomb of St Felix at Nola in Italy. There were women like Melania, the daughter and grand-daughter of consuls, who sailed to Egypt and Palestine to see the lives of hermits at first hand, before founding churches and convents in Jerusalem. And there was Marcella, the Roman matron who turned her family palace on the Aventine into a convent (see pp. 12, 22).

With such people's patronage, as well as that of the emperor and state, Christianity rose above internal tensions and took hold throughout the empire (*fig.* 3.7). Of course, there were still pagans.

**3.7** Christian wall painting from a house church in Lullingstone Villa, Kent, c.360. It shows Christians at prayer, with hands upraised in the *orantes* position. The large cross patterns on their vestments are among the earliest major depictions of the cross in Christian art.

There would even be one last great pagan emperor, Julian the Apostate, who, in the brief three years of his reign (360–63), tried in vain to turn back the clock, before being cut down on campaign in Mesopotamia. But the momentum was unstoppable.

By the last two decades of the fourth century, emperors were renouncing their traditional pagan title of *Pontifex Maximus* (Chief Priest) and enacting powerful anti-pagan legislation. In Rome, the privileges traditionally granted to the Vestal Virgins were withdrawn; pagan priests no longer received state aid; and, to cap it all, the pagan Altar of Victory, so long a symbol of Rome's might, was removed from the Senate House. Traditionalists among the senators were outraged, and a delegation was sent to the western emperor Valentinian II, in Milan, headed by the arch-pagan Symmachus. But not even his oratory was a match for the steely determination of the bishop of Milan, St Ambrose, the imperial advisor on religious affairs. Symmachus was defeated. Ambrose was ascendant.

In fact, so great by now was the power of Ambrose and the Church, that he was able repeatedly to confront the eastern emperor Theodosius, and force him several times to renounce and repent imperial decisions. Once Ambrose refused to celebrate Holy Communion until the emperor reversed his decision in a dispute between Christian and Jewish communities on the River Euphrates. Another time, when Theodosius had massacred thousands of citizens in Thessalonica following popular riots in support of a charioteer, imprisoned for committing 'unnatural practices', Ambrose ordered the emperor to do penance before he would give him Holy Communion (*fig.* 3.8).

Perhaps as a result of this experience, it was in the next year, 391, that Theodosius finally issued an edict, which outlawed pagans from sacrificing, entering temples or worshipping images. He banned the ancient art of divination. He would later make it treasonable to make offerings, to light lamps, burn incense or hang garlands at any pagan shrine. All over the empire, centuries-old practices came abruptly to an end: Greek festivals, such as the Olympic Games or the Eleusinian Mysteries, were banned; and in Rome sacrifices to the city's pagan protector,

Jupiter, were outlawed. Meanwhile, in Egypt, a group of Christian monks ran amok and, in an orgy of violence, tore down the Temple of Serapis in Alexandria.

But tensions remained. In 392, the body of Theodosius' imperial colleague in the west, Valentinian II, was found hanging in his palace. The generals claimed that the emperor's death was a suicide. Moving rapidly, as if following the timetable of a well-planned coup, they appointed the pagan Eugenius as the imperial successor. Supported by many of the surviving pagan senators, Eugenius posed a real threat not only to Theodosius' rule but also potentially to the supremacy of Christianity within the empire.

**3.8** *St Ambrose and the Emperor Theodosius*, print by Jakob Matthias Schmutzer, after Peter Paul Rubens, 1784. The scene depicts Ambrose, bishop of Milan, denying Theodosius I (r. 379–95) access to Milan Cathedral after the massacre in Thessalonica in 390.

Theodosius responded with determination. Declaring his eight-year-old son, Honorius, to be emperor of the west, he gathered an army and advanced against Eugenius in 394. The two sides met in a narrow pass by the River Frigidus in the mountains of Slovenia. Before the battle, Eugenius set up a statue of the pagan god Jupiter to inspire and protect his army. On his banners, he flaunted images of the pagan hero Hercules. On the opposing side, riding behind the standard of Christ, Theodosius led his troops, commanded by his trusted lieutenants, Stilicho and Alaric.

The battle raged long and hard. By the end of the first day, it looked as if Eugenius might win. But in the night, when fighting was suspended, Theodosius is said to have prayed for a storm. On the next morning, fierce winds raced across the valley from the east, blasting dust and sand into the faces of Eugenius' men, blinding them and breaking their resolve. Some say the wind was so strong that it turned Eugenius' arrows round and swept them back against his men.

Theodosius had won. The Christian God had triumphed. The Battle of the River Frigidus in 394 set the final seal on what the Battle of the Milvian Bridge had begun in 312.

It had taken eighty-two years to convert the Roman Empire fully to Christianity. Even half a century before, when Constantine had died in 337, there had still been a multitude of gods all jostling for attention from potential worshippers. Constantine himself had waited almost until his dying breath before committing his soul finally to the Christian God.

It was only in his last days that he had summoned to his presence a bishop to have himself baptized. And it was a strange choice of bishop, too, for he was an Arian, a follower of the theologian whom Constantine had himself cast out as a heretic. But this was not the only controversy surrounding his baptism. Years before, he had branded as heretical another sect, the Novatians, who believed that any sin committed after baptism could not be forgiven, and who therefore waited until death was near before being baptized. Had Constantine waited for the same reason? Whether Novatian or no, Constantine was baptized in Nicomedia, across the sea from his new city. Now, on his deathbed, Constantine, who had given the empire a new religion, had embraced that religion himself.

Constantine died on 22 May 337. His body was placed in a golden coffin, draped with the imperial purple and taken by ship to lie in state in the Great Palace of Constantinople. From there, in a procession led by his son, Constantius II, the coffin was taken through the city to his mausoleum, and laid in a sarcophagus of porphyry beneath the mausoleum's great dome, ringed symbolically by twelve cenotaphs for the twelve apostles. With incense and chanting, the bishops laid his soul to rest, a Christian service for a Christian emperor.

In Rome, the Senate, still predominately pagan, passed a decree proclaiming Constantine a god. Fifty-seven years later, in 394, no such decree would follow the death of Theodosius.

PART 2

# *The storm clouds gather*

# CHAPTER 4

# *Stirrings on the steppes*

*The eruption of armed men from
barbarian lands was like lava
from Mount Etna…*
(Ammianus, *Histories* XXXI.4)

A piece of horse
gear, 4th century,
probably Gothic
(see also *fig.* 4.2).

While the Roman Empire was grappling
with Christianity, upheavals of a darker kind
were boiling far to the east. Rumours started seeping through
the porous borders of the Rivers Danube and Rhine: of huge
migrations on an epic scale in the distant hinterlands of the
steppes, of strange and savage horsemen riding hard towards
the west, cutting swathes of terror in their path, while ragged
groups of terrified and harried tribesmen fled before them
(*fig.* 4.1). The Huns were on the move. Ammianus, the soldier-
historian, himself a veteran of many a campaign in eastern wars,
wrote of them in horror. They came, he says, from far away
beside a frozen sea and were incomparably cruel. Even their
appearance was chilling:

> The very moment they are born, they make deep cuts in
> their children's cheeks, so that, when hair appears in the
> course of time, its vigour might be checked by these
> furrowed scars… They have compact bodies, powerful
> limbs and thickset necks – so unnatural and terrifying to
> look at that you would think them two-leggèd beasts or
> those figures roughly hewn from tree-stumps that
> sometimes line the parapets of bridges… They wear
> clothes made out of linen or the skins of field mice sewn
> together; and, once they have put on some shabby shirt,

they will not take it off again or change it until it has
rotted away through age and fallen to pieces through
constant use. On their heads they wear round hats made
of skins, and goatskins on their hairy legs... They are
virtually joined onto their horses, which are tough but
deformed... Whatever they do by day or night, buying
or selling, eating or drinking, they do on horseback, even
leaning over their horses' narrow necks to sleep and to
enjoy such dreams as come to them... [32]

But it was their ruthlessness in battle that sowed panic in the
hearts of all they met.

When they fight they are fanatical. They ride into battle in
a wedge formation, each warrior yelling out blood-curdling
war-cries. They are lightly armed and so fast and
unpredictable that they will scatter suddenly and gallop here
and there chaotically, inflicting untold slaughter. They are so
fast that they can burst through a rampart or raid an enemy
camp before anyone has spotted them. You would rightly
say that they are the fiercest of all fighters – they can fire
missiles from far off, arrows tipped not with the usual
arrowheads but with sharp splintered bones, which they
attach onto the shafts with extraordinary skill. They fight

**4.1** View along the
River Danube from
the Roman fortress
at Salsovia (modern
Romania). 'Melting
snows meant that
the River Danube
was in flood, but the
emperor Constantius
crossed it on a bridge
of boats and so
launched an attack
on the land of
the barbarians.'
(Ammianus
Marcellinus
17.12.4, 358)

close-to without any fear for their own lives; and, while the enemy is busy watching out for sword-thrusts, they catch him with lassoes made out of plaited cloth, so that his limbs get all entangled and he cannot walk or ride.[33]

As the Hunnic hordes swept ever closer, waves of refugees began to flood into the lands beyond the limits of the Roman world, pressing hard against the barbarian tribes who lived there, forcing them ever closer to the Danube and the Rhine. The pressure on these tribes became unbearable, and by 376 reports began to reach the Roman court of throngs of barbarians massing on the farther banks of the Danube, their numbers swelling by the day, a wagon-city of desperate and displaced peoples clamouring to cross the river. And they were peoples whom the Romans knew, with whom they had done business in the past, whose men had even served as soldiers fighting for the Romans in their wars: the Visigoths.[34]

Like the Huns, the Visigoths were horsemen, but, unlike the Huns, they were skilled in agriculture and stock rearing. Tall, bearded, with long blond or red hair, and bodies swathed in skins and furs, the Goths were fearsome warriors with a proud sense of self-worth. In the 'civilized' Roman Empire, desk-bound academics, like the Greek historian Eunapius, sneered at them for being arrogant and contemptuous:

> their bodies provoked contempt in all who saw them, for they were far too big and far too heavy for their feet to carry them, and they were pinched in at the waist – just like those insects Aristotle writes of.[35]

It was a dismissive, superficial attitude widely held by Roman writers and politicians – and one that goes some way towards explaining why the Romans so often let themselves be wrong-footed: lumping together as 'barbarians' people as different as the Huns and the Goths, they underestimated and mishandled them all.

The Visigoths were the western branch of a greater Gothic tribe, who had first come into contact with the Romans three

**4.2** A set of horse gear based on Roman models, 4th century. The trappings were most likely found at Kerch in the Crimea, a region where the Goths resided at this time. The reconstruction below shows how the trappings were probably worn (see also detail, p. 54).

centuries before. At that time, they were living in what is now northeast Germany on the grasslands by the lower reaches of the River Vistula. Some time later, in the second century AD, they migrated eastwards to the Pontic Steppes, and by 230 they had settled close to the Crimea on the northwest shores of the Black Sea (*figs* 4.2–3).

It was from the Pontic Steppes that the Goths first launched their incursions into the fringes of the Roman world: initially they marched overland to Thrace; then, in their long ships, they plundered the coastal strips of the Black Sea, sailing as far south as southern Turkey. But by the final years of Constantine's reign, during the 330s, the Goths and Romans had reached an agreement. In return for peace, the Goths were settled in central-eastern Europe, in the lands of Dacia, once conquered as a Roman province, but now a useful buffer zone against the eastern barbarian tribes. Once settled north of the Danube in 332, the Goths became official allies, *foederati*, of the empire. Before long, they were joined in Dacia by Christians (from Cappadocia in Turkey), who with great energy began to convert the Goths to the new Roman religion. But the bishop converting them was an Arian. To the imperial Catholic court, the Arian brand of Christianity that the Goths began to practise was heretical.

Now, in 376, displaced by the great Hunnic migrations to the east, the Goths were massing in their many thousands on the Roman frontiers. At first the court took little notice. But gradually,

> belief in these reports became stronger, and final confirmation came with the arrival of foreign diplomats, begging that their exiled peoples might be received on our side of the river. It seemed a cause for rejoicing rather than for fear, and the experienced court-flatterers praised to the skies the great good fortune that was so unexpectedly providing the emperor with so many new recruits drawn from the very ends of the earth. They pointed out that [the barbarians], allied with his own troops, would form an invincible army. Moreover, a great quantity of gold would now pour into the treasury from annual taxes, as many provinces that had previously supplied troops would now be liable to pay tax instead.[36]

'So many new recruits…an invincible army': Ammianus' words highlight how time and again the Romans could have harnessed the Goths as a powerful allied force. Time and again, the Romans would fail to do so, instead antagonizing the Goths, until at last they were provoked to sack the ancient city.

As more and more Goths poured into their encampment on the far bank of the Danube, and as they grew increasingly desperate, Valens, the emperor of the east, at last agreed to let them into the empire. Day and night and in the driving rain the Goths crossed in boats, on rafts and in canoes hollowed out from tree trunks. So awful was their terror of what lay behind, and so intense their fervour to escape, that many tried to swim across the river, now swollen by torrential rain, fast flowing and dangerous. Many drowned, but still more came. The Romans, ever bureaucratic and efficient, tried to keep a tally of the

**4.3** A Visigothic radiate-headed copper alloy brooch with garnet-eyed bird's head knobs, dating from the 6th century. Probably worn by women, such brooches were produced by many Germanic peoples.

refugees who crossed, but even the tidy-minded Romans gave up counting in the end. The numbers were incalculable. The entire nation of the Visigoths had arrived on Roman soil.

How the Romans dealt with them was crucial. If the Goths had been settled along the Danube, given lands and been integrated within the empire, the Romans could have benefited from their manpower and labour. If the Romans had fed the hungry barbarians in the days and weeks after their desperate crossing, they might have earned their gratitude and loyalty. Instead, they treated the Goths with arrogance and cruelty, exploiting their weakness. The Romans even bartered mean rations of cheap food, stale mouldy bread and the carcasses of dogs for Gothic youths, whom they immediately enslaved (*fig. 4.4*).[37]

Eventually the vanguard of starving Goths – exhausted and disillusioned – camped outside the city of Marcianople, where the Roman generals were based, between the Danube and the sea. The Romans, unclear what to do next, invited Fritigern, the Gothic chieftain, to a banquet in the city, while outside his starving people tried repeatedly to be allowed inside the walls to buy food and provisions. Repeatedly they were denied permission and, eventually, inevitably, tempers frayed. Blows were

4.4 Detail of the Arch of Septimius Severus (193–211) in the Roman Forum showing soldiers leading captured Parthians after Severus' victory in Mesopotamia in 198. 'Severus killed many men and earned the title Parthicus.' (*Scriptores Historiae Augustae, Severus* 16)

exchanged. The violence escalated. Roman soldiers made arrests. The Goths retaliated and the situation spiralled wildly out of control. When news reached the generals, they slaughtered the Gothic bodyguard within the city and tried to hold Fritigern as hostage; but, when Fritigern insisted that he could calm his people if he returned to them, they set him free. Reunited with his warriors and shaken by his hosts' duplicity, Fritigern vowed vengeance. From being Rome's grateful allies, the Goths had turned into her implacable enemies. Now they unleashed their fury.

Villas, villages and towns – whatever lay before them – were pillaged and burned. The province was in turmoil. A Roman army was sent out. It was annihilated and its arms and armour plundered. Elsewhere, provincials, who had grown suspicious of the Gothic regiments already serving loyally in the Roman army, refused to give them the supplies they needed and threatened them instead. The soldiers responded. Blood was shed. The Goths went over to the enemy.

As the weeks and months dragged on, the whole of Scythia and Moesia and Thrace descended into anarchy. Battle followed battle as the Roman army tried to regain some order, but again and again they were unsuccessful as the Goths swept across the province, leaving burning villages and empty farms in their wake. Crucially, though, the Goths knew little of siege warfare and left fortified cities alone.

> Fritigern announced that he had no quarrel with city walls, but rather urged his followers to attack, without risk, any rich and fertile regions that lay still unprotected… Their innate confidence was greatly bolstered by the fact that, with every day that went by, their numbers were swollen by great hordes of their own people, who had previously been enslaved; many, too, who had been traded – for a little watery wine or mouldy bread – by [their own] people, who were almost dead from hunger after crossing the river… The whole country was ablaze with fire and slaughter that made no allowances for age or sex.[38]

The empire's Balkan provinces lay in unfettered turmoil. Eventually Valens, emperor of the east, arrived at the head of a fresh army in Constantinople. A swarthy man, bow-legged, with a paunch and able to see clearly out of one eye only, Valens was now fifty years old (*fig.* 4.5). Although his propagandists painted him as a tough and rugged man, he was, in fact, averse to hardship, preferring a life of luxury and ease. He had one other major weak spot – he was intensely jealous of the western emperor, his young nephew, Gratian.

For some time, reports had been coming back to Valens of Gratian's victories on the Rhine. Here, too, barbarian tribes were on the march, and in February 378, as many as 40,000 Alamanni crossed the frozen river, causing panic in the German provinces. Gratian led his troops against the barbarians and, in a hard-fought battle, drove them back across the river, pursuing them deep into the heartland of their territory before wheeling back across the border, where he energetically imposed order once more on his stricken lands. And now he was marching towards Constantinople to the aid of his uncle, Valens.

But rather than wait for him, Valens was determined to fight alone. He did not want to share the glory of his victory over the Goths with Gratian. He did not wish to be eclipsed. Instead, he led his forces to the town of Hadrianople, near which, reports assured him, a small section of the enemy were camped. While Valens was preparing for battle, a delegation led by a Christian priest arrived from the Gothic camp. Terms were offered: peace in exchange for land and food. But there was more. The priest,

**4.5** Gold *solidus* of Valens (r. 364–78), struck at Siscia (Sisak in Croatia) in 364–7. In hindsight the design seems ironic, as the inscription proclaims the 'well-being of the state' while the emperor holds a Christian standard and kicks a barbarian. In reality, Valens died at the hands of the Goths, along with most of his field army, at the Battle of Hadrianople.

a close and trusted confidant of Fritigern, gave the emperor a private letter from the Gothic king (who was most adept in treachery and in deceit of every kind). In the letter, [Fritigern] spoke of Valens as his future friend and ally. But he went on to say that he would not be able to contain his people's savagery nor persuade them to make terms conducive to the Romans, unless he could point out Valens' troops, close by and armed …which would strike fear in their hearts and constrain their lust for war.[39]

Valens was unconvinced. The delegation was sent back empty-handed.

It was a pattern that would repeat itself with predictable and baffling regularity over the next thirty years: a Gothic commander offering loyalty in exchange for land; a Roman emperor, over-confident and suspicious, rejecting terms out of hand; the final bloody outcome.

On 9 August 378, the sun rose in a cloudless sky as Valens led his troops from Hadrianople. Eight Roman miles[40] they marched in full armour over rough terrain, as the day grew ever hotter and the sun baked down. As they approached the Gothic camp, their eyes began to water and their throats to sting, as the acrid smell of smoke grew ever stronger. The enemy had set the countryside on fire. In the scorching heat the smoke choked men and animals alike, parching and exhausting them.

At last the sound of wild barbaric war-cries, faint at first, then louder, filled the heavy air, and the scouts reported that the Goths were indeed close, encamped within a massive circle of wagons on the hill ahead. The Roman generals marshalled their exhausted men. Again a delegation of Goths arrived, apparently seeking peace. Again they were sent back, this time on the pretext that the Gothic delegates were too lowly in rank to do business with Valens. Another envoy came and suggested an exchange of hostages while Fritigern himself would meet with the emperor. At last the Romans seemed prepared to talk, but the man chosen to head the hostages refused to play his part. In the delay that followed, disaster struck.

Without waiting for orders, a group of Roman archers opened fire on the Gothic camp. Immediately the Goths responded with their cavalry, galloping out from between the wagons, routing the Romans and slaughtering everyone in their path. The Romans regrouped and fought back. Their left wing forced the churning mass of Goths back to their wagon camp, but they could go no further:

> Abandoned by the rest of the cavalry, and forced back by the sheer pressure of enemy numbers, it [the left wing] collapsed like a broken dyke. The infantry stood unprotected and so tightly crowded together that a man could scarcely raise his sword or draw his arm back again. Such a cloud of dust was raised that the sky was hidden from sight. Hideous screams filled the air. On all sides, missiles rained down, each hitting its target, each deadly. No one could see the missiles before they struck. No one could escape them. As the barbarians poured down in countless numbers, they overwhelmed the baggage trains and trampled our men underfoot. An orderly retreat became impossible. Our men became ever more densely crushed together and hemmed in, with no hope of escape.[41]

It was a bloodbath. When night eventually fell and the Goths returned to their encampment, the few surviving Romans stumbled blindly back to Hadrianople. It was only in the next few days that they realized their emperor had not returned with them. Hacked down alongside his men, his body lay anonymous and unidentified, one among countless others who had fallen in the worst defeat endured by the Roman army in almost 600 years.[42]

It was a disaster of catastrophic proportions, a self-inflicted wound, which, if not mortal, was near crippling. Rome's eastern army had been destroyed by an enemy of its own making, by a people who had offered friendship and alliance, by refugees who could have helped the Romans face the Hunnic hordes already closing in from the Steppes.

In response, Gratian acted with decisiveness and energy. He brought out of self-imposed exile one of the greatest generals and tacticians of his age – the thirty-two-year-old Theodosius –

and appointed him co-*Augustus*, emperor of the east, in 379.

In the years that followed, Theodosius pursued the Goths throughout the eastern provinces and Balkans, as they cut a swathe of devastation through Pannonia and Thrace and then south into Greece. At last, in 382, with Fritigern now dead, Theodosius made a treaty settling the Goths along the southern Danube frontier, where they were allowed great latitude in governing themselves. At the same time, he enlisted Gothic warriors into the Roman army, some as regulars and some as *foederati*, allied troops who could be called upon to fight when help was needed (*fig.* 4.6).

But in 383, almost before the seal was set on the treaty with the Goths, news reached Theodosius that Gratian was dead. For some time, Gratian had been unpopular in the west. Despite his brilliance and energy, he had 'an innate tendency to play the fool',[43] and had increasingly given himself over to hunting and pleasure. His appearance, in full Gothic costume, at an event soon after the Battle of Hadrianople had angered his troops. In protest,

**4.6** Relief from the base of an Egyptian obelisk erected by Theodosius in the Circus (Hippodrome) at Constantinople in 390. The relief shows Theodosius and his retinue seated in the imperial box above suppliant Goths. An inscription proclaims: 'All things yield to Theodosius and to his everlasting descendents...'

Part 2 The storm clouds gather

the Roman army in Britain – already under pressure from attacks along its northern border – had rebelled and appointed its own man, Magnus Maximus, as emperor in 383. Deserted by his troops, Gratian fled to Lyons, where he was betrayed by the governor, and killed by the enemy.

For another five years, Theodosius and Gratian's successor, Valentinian II, faced the troops of the rebel emperor Magnus Maximus in Gaul, while all the time the empire's borders strained under the pressure of the barbarian tribes outside. Victory against the rebels in 388 allowed Theodosius to attend more fully to the problem of the Goths, whom he now desperately tried to integrate into both the army and society at large.

But a crux occurred in 390, with the massacre of spectators in the circus at Thessalonica. Riots had broken out when the commander of the Gothic garrison had imprisoned a popular charioteer on a charge of lewd behaviour. In the violence that followed, the garrison commander was killed. In a bid to reassert authority and bring the city back under control, Theodosius ordered the garrison into the circus to butcher the protesters gathered there. One Church chronicler observed:

> They say that seven thousand died without recourse to law and without any sentence being passed against them, but they were all cut down indiscriminately like ears of wheat at harvest time.[44]

Goths had been ordered by the emperor to kill Roman citizens. It was, indeed, a new social order, very different from the world of only twelve years before. In disgust, Ambrose, bishop of Milan, refused Theodosius Holy Communion.

But it was another of Theodosius' decisions that would have an even more profound effect upon the future shape of Rome. As the Goths proved themselves an ever more crucial force in the eastern Roman army, Theodosius at some stage raised one of them to military command: their unusually gifted warrior and leader, Alaric, whose name meant 'Lord of All'. Alaric first made his mark in history fighting loyally for his emperor at the Battle of the River Frigidus in 394, where he led his men fearlessly into the thick of the fighting (see p. 51). For him, the carnage at Frigidus would prove a turning point. For on that day a disproportionate number of Goths fell on the battlefield; and the feeling soon took hold among the surviving few that they had been deliberately sent into the fiercest action. Why? Because they were dispensable, because their lives were cheaper than those of their Roman comrades. But, for as long as Theodosius remained in power, Alaric and the Goths stood firmly by their oaths of loyalty to the emperor. Once he was dead, it was another matter.

And death came only five months later. On 17 January 395, Theodosius, by now the undisputed ruler of both eastern and western empires, lay dangerously ill in the imperial palace in Milan. By his bedside stood his chief of staff, the brilliant young general Stilicho, whose very pedigree seemed to encapsulate the new world of Rome.

Born in Germany of a Vandal father and a Roman mother, Stilicho straddled two traditions, Roman and barbarian. Educated and clever, he had risen through the ranks; and, after a successful diplomatic mission to the Persian Empire, he had been appointed a general. Indeed, so close was he to Theodosius that the emperor had given his niece, Serena, to be his bride.

Now, as Theodosius lay dying, a conversation passed between emperor and general that would define the boundaries of Roman power for the next decade and more. When the doors swung open and Stilicho strode out, he made two proclamations. The first was that the emperor was dead; the second, that the emperor's dying wish had been for Stilicho himself to act as regent in the west during the minority of Theodosius' younger son, Honorius; at the same time, Stilicho was to serve as protector to Theodosius' elder son, Arcadius, emperor of the east. According to Stilicho, Theodosius had bequeathed him supreme power over the entire Roman world.

# CHAPTER 5

# *Stilicho ascendant*

*It is recorded that Theodosius' sons succeeded him as emperor. But if one were to give a truer picture of what happened (and truth is, after all, the purpose of history), they took the title of emperors, while in reality total power lay with Rufinus in the east and Stilicho in the west. So the emperors were controlled by their regents, who, as if they were themselves the emperors, were constantly fighting each other – not in open warfare, but rather using the clandestine arts of treachery and deception.* (Eunapius, fr. 62)

Portrait detail of Stilicho (d. 408) from an ivory diptych, c.395–400 (see also *fig.* 5.5).

In Milan, Stilicho's protectorate was greeted with enthusiasm. In Constantinople it was rejected out of hand. For in the east a new court had already grown up around Arcadius, Theodosius' elder son (*fig.* 5.1). Now seventeen years old, Arcadius had been (in name at least) emperor of the east since he was six; and in that time he had attracted around him a powerful group of advisors led by the ambitious praetorian prefect, Rufinus, who had no intention of ceding any power to Stilicho. Instead, he sought to strengthen his own position by marrying his daughter to the emperor Arcadius.

But his plan failed, thwarted by bitter enemies at court, chief among whom was the eunuch Eutropius, who was utterly determined to undermine and eventually oust Rufinus. Zosimus, the great Byzantine historian – himself a member of the eastern court three generations later – describes how Eutropius set to work. First, he tempted Arcadius with a description of a highborn girl of extraordinary beauty.

**5.1** Gold *solidus* of Arcadius (r. 383–408) struck at Constantinople, c.403–8. The facing helmeted bust heralds designs commonly used on later Byzantine coins. The reverse shows Victory, with the inscription 'New Hope for the State'.

When Eutropius saw that the emperor was intrigued by his account [of the girl], he showed him a painting of her, which increased Arcadius' enthusiasm even more, and persuaded him to choose her for his wife. Rufinus knew nothing of these goings-on, believing instead that his own daughter would soon marry the emperor, while he himself would soon share the empire. When Eutropius saw that his marriage plans had worked, he commanded the whole populace to dance, bearing garlands as if for a royal wedding. Taking with him the imperial robes and other trimmings (carried by the palace staff), he paraded through the centre of the city, accompanied by all the people. Everyone running along beside the bearers believed that the gifts were for Rufinus' daughter, but when they came to [the house where the girl was staying], Eutropius and his men took the gifts inside, making it plain who would be marrying the emperor.[45]

Eutropius had cleverly achieved his aim. The girl, Aelia Eudoxia, married Arcadius in 395 (*fig.* 5.2). But, far from being a cipher of Eutropius, she would become one of the most powerful figures in the east.

If Rufinus had been thwarted in his dynastic plans, Stilicho was not. He moved quickly to betroth his young daughter, Maria, to the ten-year-old Honorius, who would marry her three years later. At the ceremony the wedding song, composed

**5.2** Gold *solidus* of Aelia Eudoxia (wife of Arcadius), struck at Constantinople, c.400–2. She is shown being crowned with a diadem by the Hand of God. On the reverse, Victory inscribes the Chi-Rho symbol on a shield, proclaiming the 'Good Condition of the State'.

by the court poet Claudian, included an imaginative portrayal of the young emperor in the days before his engagement, described in the somewhat disingenuous lines:

> Honorius was consumed by fires of passion for the promised maiden... and burned with the fervency of first love. He knew not where his fervour came from, nor what his deep sighs meant; and yet, still inexperienced in love, he knew the feelings overwhelming him... He asked himself: 'How much longer will the great Stilicho withhold from me my prayers? Why does he delay a marriage he has approved already? Why does he refuse to grant my chaste desires?'[46]

Chaste, indeed, were Honorius' desires. Neither with Maria, nor with her sister Thermantia, whom he married after her death, would he have any children. He may have been as disinterested in, or as incapable of, fathering an heir as he was of ruling his empire.

But there was little time for either of the courts to spend in celebrating marriages. Like the uninvited guest of myth, who sows discord at the wedding feast, there was a baleful presence at the heart of the empire, and he was harbouring a grudge. Alaric felt cheated. He had led his Goths into the fiercest fighting at the Battle of the River Frigidus in defence of

Rome. The least he felt he could expect was to be made a general, an appointment that would have guaranteed supplies and status for his men. But the appointment did not come, and Alaric was not amused.

Yet, although he felt sidelined by the Romans, he was lionized by his own people. Shortly after the Battle of Hadrianople in 378, the king of the Goths, Athanaric, had died. For many years the Goths had had no single ruler. Now, in 395, in the great tribal assembly by the banks of the River Danube, they came together to choose a new king. Their choice was Alaric. According to one Church historian, he was 'of good pedigree, being of the family of the Balthi. A long time before, they had been given the name "Baltha", which means "Brave", because of their great courage.'

The historian's next sentence is short but pregnant with significance: 'When Alaric was proclaimed king, he held an assembly of his people and persuaded them to seek a kingdom through their own endeavours instead of passively serving others.'[47]

So the Goths packed their belongings in their wagons, and began their trek in search of a homeland.

In Constantinople, Rufinus heard the news. He was still smarting from his failure to secure his daughter's marriage to Arcadius, still trying to steal a march on Stilicho, still desperate to be the saviour of the eastern empire, and to be seen to have saved it. So he entered into secret negotiations with Alaric, urging him to bypass Constantinople and go with all haste west, where lay rich pickings, all unprotected. West they went, avoiding any of Rufinus' lands, and bringing terror to the rest. A hundred years later, the historian Zosimus could still see the scars left in the wake of the Goths:

> Alaric left Thrace and marched through Macedonia and Thessaly, destroying everything in his path. When he came close to Thermopylae, he sent a messenger secretly to Antiochus, the proconsul, and Gerontius, the garrison commander, to announce his approach. Gerontius and his

garrison withdrew, affording the barbarians free and unopposed passage into Greece. At once they went about ravaging fields and destroying cities, slaughtering the men and carrying off all the women and children as well as all the country's wealth. All Boeotia and the rest of Greece through which the barbarians passed were so devastated that to this day they show the signs of the disaster.[48]

According to Zosimus, who was clearly not unbiased, this was all somehow part of Rufinus' master plan to consolidate his powerbase in Constantinople, where the court was in a state of panic (*fig.* 5.3). But the plan, if plan there was, did not include Stilicho.

Although Greece was part of the eastern empire, Stilicho in the west could not sit idly by and watch the Goths come ever closer unopposed. Instead, he landed in the south of Greece and harried the barbarians, forcing them first into the mountains of Arcadia, then north to Epirus (modern Albania). Why he did not follow up his victories remains a puzzle. According to Zosimus, Stilicho was too busy devoting himself to 'luxury, comic actors and shameless women', but somehow Zosimus' portrayal of Stilicho as an indolent playboy does not sit comfortably with other accounts of his wily ambition. Instead, it is more likely that he was ordered out of the eastern empire by the government at Constantinople. Certainly, this is implied by what happened next.

**5.3** A view east across the Bosphorus towards Turkey from the European part of Istanbul (modern Constantinople). The city's position afforded good communications to the west and east; and, when under siege in later centuries, it was able to take in supplies from the sea.

No sooner had Stilicho returned to Italy than he despatched to Constantinople a detachment of soldiers, sanctioned by Honorius and commanded by Gainas, himself a Goth in the Roman army. Although sent ostensibly as reinforcements for the garrison, in reality their mission was murder.

When they were near the city, Gainas sent a message to the emperor Arcadius, requesting that he welcome the troops at an official ceremony in their honour.

> The emperor was persuaded to come out before the city. Rufinus, the city prefect, accompanied him. But, once Gainas and his men had prostrated themselves and received due welcome from the emperor, Gainas gave the signal. All at once they surrounded Rufinus, falling on him with their swords. One sliced off his right hand, another his left, while another cut off his head and ran off singing a victory song. Their mockery was so extreme that they carried his hand all round the city, asking anyone they met to give a donation to 'The Insatiable One'.[49]

Yet the assassination of Rufinus in 395 did nothing to improve relations between Stilicho and the east. Instead, it served only to undermine them further. For the eunuch Eutropius had been biding his time. Now he effortlessly slid into the mantle left by Rufinus.

Few figures of the age have inspired such vivid writing as Eutropius. One of his contemporaries, an academic, tells how 'the eunuch ruled in the palace, and, like a very serpent, coiled his way round every office, throttling everything'.[50] Similarly, an ancient dictionary entry describes how most shrank in fear from the eunuch's prying ears, although he did inspire some imitators:

> even some who were already grown men, craving to be eunuchs and yearning to become Eutropiuses, disposed of both their sense and their testicles that they might enjoy the condition of Eutropius. Gold statues of him appeared everywhere, and he erected dazzling palaces more resplendent than the entire city.[51]

Meanwhile, in Italy, Stilicho's court poet, Claudian, went to town on the eunuch. His 500-line poem *Against Eutropius* (399) drips with vitriol, with vivid descriptions of his castration and debauchery. But the picture he paints of Eutropius' physical appearance tops it all:

Already his skin sagged with age, and his face, more wrinkled than a raisin, was furrowed by the deep grooves on his cheeks – deeper than the furrows in the golden cornfields, cut by the deep-pressed plough, or than the folds of ships' sails flapping in the wind. Repulsive grubs gnawed at his head. Bare patches of his scalp showed where his hair had fallen out, like wisps of dry dead corn, which struggle on a cracked, parched field, or like a moulting swallow that sits dying on a tree in winter, shedding its feathers in the icy cold… His pallor and cadaverous appearance disgusted his masters, and his anaemic face and emaciated form repelled all who met him, frightening the children, sickening everyone who dined with him, shaming fellow-slaves, an ill-omen to any who crossed his path.[52]

The historian Zosimus concludes that Eutropius was

drunk with wealth. He imagined he was floating on the clouds. His spies were almost everywhere, keeping everyone under surveillance and gathering information about what each person was doing. There was nothing from which he did not profit… No one in all of Constantinople dared look Eutropius in the face. He had only Stilicho in the west to contend with.[53]

Eutropius quickly moved to undermine his western rival. First, he made a pact with Alaric. Giving in to his demands for land and status, he allowed the Goths officially to settle Dacia,[54] while at the same time granting Alaric the post of general. Then he turned the screw on Stilicho. At a meeting of the Senate at Constantinople, Eutropius levelled charges against Stilicho, pointing out that he had led his army into Greece, one of the eastern provinces, in his campaign against Alaric. But it did not really matter what the charges were. Eutropius already had the Senate sewn up. Its vote was a foregone conclusion. It declared Stilicho a public enemy.

The next move in the power game was played out in Africa, the province on which Italy and Rome depended for its food supplies. Eutropius persuaded its commander, Gildo, that since Stilicho had been branded a public enemy, sanctions should be imposed on him and the lands he governed. The food supplies should be cut off – in fact, they should be diverted to Constantinople and the east.

In truth, faced with a senatorial decree, Gildo had little choice. He acquiesced to everything. Supplies to Italy dried up in 397. In the east, Eutropius sat back and waited, convinced that it was only a matter of time before Stilicho was forced to capitulate.

But Stilicho was a master of politics. Ever since he had found himself in power, he had been courting the western Senate and the people of Rome, partly by pardoning the pagan senators who had supported Eugenius against Theodosius at the Battle of the River Frigidus. Chief among them was Symmachus, with whom Stilicho corresponded regularly, and who had once argued with Bishop Ambrose over the removal of the Altar of Victory from the Senate House (*fig.* 5.4). Meanwhile Stilicho had also ensured that the urban populace of Rome was well fed and well entertained. Then, in a masterstroke of constitutional politics, he used the Senate to strike back at Eutropius once and for all.

For Stilicho was well aware that, in any dispute between the eastern and western Senates, Rome could override Constantinople. The loophole was created back in 330, when Constantine I had inaugurated the new Senate of Constantinople (see pp. 46–7). Stilicho now challenged Constantinople's decree that he was a public enemy; and the Roman Senate passed its own ruling. Not only did it brand Eutropius himself a public enemy; it declared war on Gildo.

**5.4** This ivory leaf from a diptych was used as a book or document cover, normally for presentation purposes (see also *fig.* 2.5). It was apparently commissioned by the Symmachi family in Rome to commemorate Quintus Aurelius Symmachus (c.340–402), a great pagan orator and opponent of Christianity. The ivory probably shows Symmachus as consul, riding in an elephant-drawn carriage. His soul is represented by two eagles flying up from the pyre, from where he is taken to heaven by winged figures, watched by the Roman sun god Sol and five ancestors.

For the first time in many years, the Roman Senate was regaining power and it savoured the sensation. Claudian, as always, was on hand to immortalize the occasion in leaden verse:

> The avenging army did not sail until the Senate had given their approval for the war, as was their ancient right. Stilicho reintroduced this practice, which had been neglected for so long, that the senators should command the generals to fight...[55]

In fact, there was a personal dimension to the expedition against Gildo. It was led by his brother, Mascezel, with whom Gildo had quarrelled ('like a crazy barbarian', as Zosimus tellingly puts it) and whose sons he had killed. The expedition was a success. Mascezel prevailed; Gildo hanged himself; and the province was restored to Rome under the governorship of Bathanarius, Stilicho's brother-in-law.

But the story has a sinister sequel.

> Gildo's brother came back to Italy in triumph. But Stilicho resented his glory (although to his face he appeared to flatter him, which led Mascezel to entertain high hopes). Then one day, on a bridge outside the city, Stilicho gave a signal to his guards, who pushed Mascezel... off the bridge and into the river. Stilicho laughed as Mascezel was swept away by the current and drowned.[56]

It may be that this story was the product of Eutropius' propaganda machine. Zosimus described the enmity between Stilicho and Eutropius:

> From now on, the hatred between Eutropius and Stilicho was no longer hidden. Everyone was talking about it. But although they hated one other, they shared one thing in common: they relished the misery of those they ruled. Stilicho married his daughter Maria to the emperor Honorius, while Eutropius kept Arcadius like a fattened animal.[57]

In fact, Eutropius himself would not survive much longer. Blamed for a disastrous campaign against the Ostrogoths in Asia Minor, he was powerless in the face of accusations levelled against him by Gainas and Arcadius' wife, the empress Eudoxia. He was dragged from the church in which he had sought sanctuary and arrested. In Rome, the episode inspired Claudian to compose another poem (600 lines this time), which began with the measured observation: 'Fortune, tired of her mad joke, has thrown him down from his high post and returned him to his former life.'[58]

After months in captivity during which he was shipped off to Cyprus and then back again, Eutropius was eventually killed.

For a time, Stilicho, Honorius and the western empire enjoyed a period of comparative tranquillity, boosted by a certain sense of *schadenfreude*, which grew with each report that came from the east, where Gainas was causing mayhem. Accusations of collusion with the enemy had been levelled against him after his failure to contain the Ostrogoths in Asia Minor; the citizens of Constantinople had rioted; the empress Eudoxia had withdrawn her support; and 7,000 of his men had been corralled into a church and killed. With his remaining troops, Gainas had fled across the Danube, where he was butchered by the Huns. His head was sent back to Arcadius as a diplomatic gift. Meanwhile, on 9 January 400, Eudoxia was elevated to *Augusta*, on a par with her husband, the political mistress of the eastern world.

It was an appointment that heralded a reign, if not of terror, then of suspicion:

> Informers were rife as never before, always fawning on the
> eunuchs of the court... The emperor was the worst kind
> of fool, and his wife, who was very headstrong, even for
> a woman, was devoted to those who controlled her, the
> omnipresent grasping eunuchs, and her ladies-in-waiting.
> She made life so unbearable for everyone that to the
> average person nothing was preferable to death.[59]

**5.5** Ivory diptych, c.395–400, showing Stilicho, his wife Serena and son Eucherius. Stilicho is dressed as a soldier, Serena as a Roman matron holding a rose. Both Stilicho and Eucherius wear distinctive late Roman crossbow brooches on their shoulders. The ivory actually honours Eucherius who holds a diptych, which confers on him an honorary title (see also detail, p. 67).

The same year, 400, saw Stilicho's star rise ever higher, too. Appointed consul, the most powerful official post to which he could aspire, he was fêted by the people. Claudian went into paroxysms, pouring out a torrent of purple poetry praising Stilicho, comparing him to every Roman hero he could think of. In official artworks, too, the semi-barbarian Stilicho was being portrayed as a Roman through-and-through, appearing on exquisite ivory diptyches, with his wife and son – an honour reserved exclusively for the emperor and members of the very highest echelons of the Establishment *(fig. 5.5)*.

But the peace in the west was not to last. The pressures building up, both internally and on the borders, had reached breaking point. The levees were about to collapse and the empire to be inundated by a flood of crises, which would change its face forever.

Part 2 The storm clouds gather

# CHAPTER 6

# *Implosion*

*It seems man is more likely to slip and stumble in times of good fortune than in times of adversity.*
(Eunapius, fr. 57)

It was Alaric who made the first move sometime in 401. Not content with the lands he had been granted in Illyricum, and encouraged perhaps by the eastern court, he called a meeting of his elders. It was time, he said, to move on. It was time to cross to Italy.

Detail of a sailing ship from a wall mosaic in the the church of St Apollinaire Nuovo at Ravenna, late 5th or early 6th century (see also *fig.* 6.1).

Scant details survive of what happened next or why. Much of the evidence comes from the dense and effusive poetry of Claudian. He describes a later assembly of Alaric's 'Senate' of 'longhaired Gothic elders, swathed in animal skins, their faces marked by many battle scars. Infirm, they stood supported not by walking-sticks but by their spears. It was as if Old Age itself, still armed and ready, had propped itself up on their long pikes.'[60]

Alaric, like some ancient pagan warlord, is said to have told the assembly how the gods themselves had urged him on.

No dreams for me, no flights of birds; no, but a voice that issued clear and unequivocally from the sacred grove: 'No more delaying, Alaric! Quick! Cross the Alps this very year and you will reach the city.' So far, the journey has been rendered easy for me. So, what man now would be so sluggish as to doubt or shrink back from obeying the summons of the gods?[61]

For some time the great migration moved on unopposed. By winter 401, the Goths were camped in the region of Venetia in

**6.1** Wall mosaic in the church of St Apollinaire Nuovo at Ravenna, built in the late 5th or early 6th century during the period of Ostrogothic rule in Italy. It shows the walled city of Ravenna with ships in its port at Classe (see also detail, p. 79).

northern Italy. In the spring of the next year they marched against Milan. For some time, Milan had been the seat of the western court. With its baths, its Christian basilicas, its circus and palaces, it was a centre not only of government but also of culture: home to the most skilled silversmiths and specialists in ivory. But it was also a fortified city, built to withstand attack. Nonetheless, despite the city's massive ramparts and great defensive towers, the court was terrified by the impending Gothic onslaught. For one thing, Stilicho was not within easy reach in Italy, having been called away to the Danube far away, where the Ostrogoths under their king, Radagaisus, had breached the empire's borders. For another, no one knew how long Milan could withstand a siege.

Rather than wait to find out, the imperial court hurriedly packed essentials and, with the imperial guard on high alert, conducted the emperor Honorius and his wife, Maria, eastwards to Ravenna, a city built in swampland by the Adriatic Sea (*fig.* 6.1). Since the time of Augustus, the first Roman emperor,

Ravenna had been an important naval base, with its port
of Classe harbouring the fleet operating in the eastern
Mediterranean. More than a hundred years later, Ravenna
was described as being:

> closed in like an island by the ebb and flow of waters.
> To the east is the sea... but on the west is marshland
> penetrated by only one very narrow entrance. To the
> north is a branch of the River Po... To the south is the
> main river, a seventh part of which has been diverted by
> the emperor Augustus to form a very wide canal, which
> flows through the middle of the city, providing a most
> pleasant harbour at its mouth... The city itself glories in
> three names, just as it boasts a three-fold location. The
> closest part is called Ravenna, the furthest Classe, and
> in between the city and the sea lies Caesarea, a most
> luxurious place with a fine sandy beach, truly excellent
> for riding.[62]

With its houses, palaces and churches built on a network of islands, or on piles sunk deep into the marshy soil, Ravenna had a curiously liminal, shifting atmosphere all of its own (*fig. 6.2*). More importantly, its towering walls were designed to withstand a siege. And if the worst did come, the fleet lay at anchor close by, ready for a swift escape.

But for the moment, escape was unnecessary. While the emperor and his courtiers were still settling into their new apartments by the sea, they heard the news that they had been hoping for. By early 402 Stilicho had defeated Radagaisus on the Danube, and was marching home. Troops had been summoned back from Britain to assist him against Alaric. Stilicho was safely back in Italy. Milan had been saved. And now the Goths were fleeing west towards the Alps.

On 6 April 402, Stilicho caught up with the Goths at Pollentia. It was Easter Sunday, a day on which Christian Romans would not fight, or so the Christian Goths believed. They were wrong. Stilicho's men launched a surprise attack against the Gothic camp and, in the panic and confusion, captured Alaric's wife and family.

**6.2** The Neonian Baptistry is the oldest surviving building in Ravenna, dating to the late 4th or early 5th century. It was built at the time of Archbishop Ursus (Orso), but was named after Archbishop Neone, who commissioned mosaics inside the building in the mid-5th century.

Part 2 The storm clouds gather

The Goths regrouped and for a while continued to make inroads into northern Italy, until in the next year, 403, Stilicho won another victory outside Verona. But losses had been heavy on both sides, and a treaty seemed the best way forward. It was probably now that Alaric's family was returned to him. Whatever the deal, it left both sides with some traces of honour. Alaric led his army out of Italy, back east to Illyricum; Stilicho received the adulation of the Roman people.

Italy was ablaze with pomp and ceremony. Coins specially struck to celebrate the victory showed Honorius trampling a Goth, or towering over a barbarian captive, the inscriptions proclaiming a 'Victorious Augustus', 'Triumphant Over A Barbarian People' (fig. 6.3).

**6.3** Silver medallion of Honorius struck at Rome, early in the period 404–8. The reverse proclaims Honorius triumphant over the barbarian people, symbolized by a seated captive. The coin was almost certainly struck to celebrate Stilicho's defeat of Alaric in 402/3.

It was against the background of such great jubilations, in 404, that Stilicho and nineteen-year-old Honorius (now in his sixth consulship) made their triumphant entry into Rome, with the devoted court poet Claudian at their side. In his poem to mark the occasion, Claudian surpassed even himself, describing how the women of Rome adulated Honorius. They could not tear their eyes away from his 'rosy cheeks' and 'diadem-encircled hair', his fine head, 'as handsome as the god Bacchus', adorned with 'strings of Red Sea emeralds'; nor his 'strapping shoulders' and limbs 'swathed in the robes of state' and 'jewels of jasper':

A coy young girl blushed with modesty as she gazed at Honorius, and asked her aged nurse: 'What do those dragon-standards mean? Do they just flutter in the wind, or are they really hissing, poised to snatch their enemies between their jaws?' Then, when she saw the knights in their chain mail astride their bronze-armoured horses, she exclaimed: 'Where do they come from, these men of iron?

What land created these horses of metal?'… Fear mingled with joy as she pointed at the peacock feathers on the soldiers' crested helmets; and glimpsed a flash of red silk rippling across the horses' shoulders from beneath their golden armour.

This was Fortune's reward, for all your labours, Stilicho: to see riding beside you in his chariot your son-in-law Honorius, in the flower of his youth, passing through the streets of Rome in triumph; and to remember in your heart that day when, in the midst of terror and confusion, a dying father entrusted his son to your care.[63]

The less excited in the crowd might have asked why Stilicho had allowed the Goths, now safely back in Illyricum, to slip through his fingers, why he had not annihilated Alaric when he had the chance. They might have wondered, too, if the latest rumours were true: had Stilicho made a secret pact with Alaric to join forces in attacking the east and overthrowing Arcadius…?

Before anyone could check the truth of the rumours, Stilicho was soon being challenged again by another Gothic chieftain he had failed sufficiently to subjugate – his old foe Radagaisus. Even as the triumph over Alaric was being celebrated on the streets of Rome in 404, Radagaisus was planning a come-back. In late 405, he and his people swarmed south across the Danube and the Alps. Before the Romans could react, the Goths were back in Italy.

This new wave of barbarians, coming so close on the heels of Alaric, caused panic. Not even Rome felt safe. Quickly the government passed emergency measures. Citizens were offered higher rates of pay, and slaves their freedom, to encourage them to join the depleted army, while Stilicho desperately cast around for any troops he could find. Eventually, with a force including auxiliaries drawn from the Huns, he forced Radagaisus to raise his siege of Florence and retreat to the hills of Fiesole. In the desperate battle that ensued in August 406, Radagaisus himself was killed. Twelve thousand of his men surrendered and were immediately drafted into the Roman army. But by now time was beginning to run out for Stilicho. At the fringes of the empire, security, already fragile, was disintegrating at an alarming rate as raids and incursions stretched the border troops to breaking point.

The past winter on the western fringes had been harsh, with blizzards driving hard across most of northern Europe. Roads had been blocked and lines of communication cut. Now news of a threat, which somehow reached even Britain, brought an icy chill of its own. On New Year's Eve, 406, an incalculable multitude of people, vast tribes of Vandals, Alans, Suevi and Burgundii had crossed the frozen Rhine, all fleeing from the fast-approaching Hun. Now, with the thawing of the snow and the coming of spring, the barbarians fanned out west and south through Germany and into Gaul, pillaging and slaughtering, and setting fire to every house, town and city in their path. A Christian bishop would later write of how 'the skies were thick with smoke as all of Gaul burned on one pyre.'[64]

Meanwhile, on the farther reaches of the empire, Britain, already weakened by the withdrawal of the troops, which had been summoned back to Italy to combat Alaric in 402, found itself attacked on all sides by the Saxons, Picts and Scots (*fig. 6.4*).

**6.4** A hoard of Roman hack-silver and coins buried at Coleraine, Northern Ireland, early 5th century. The latest coins date from the reign of Constantine III (407–11). The stash was either loot taken by Irish raiders in Roman Britain, or possibly payment to Irish mercenaries serving in the late Roman army.

As the frequency of attacks increased, the generals in Britain grew ever more angry and frustrated. The central command in Italy, faced with problems close to home, seemed to have forgotten them. They felt that they had been cut adrift. The only course left, they reasoned, was to declare an emperor of their own. After some dispute and two abortive attempts, the army in Britain finally declared a candidate behind whom they could all unite. Early in 407, they elected as their emperor an officer who not only had the auspicious name of Constantine, but was also charismatic and decisive. Faced with such a looming crisis, he knew immediately what he had to do. To save Gaul, he must abandon Britain. And so it was that the last significant body of Roman troops put to sea and sailed across the English Channel, never to return.

News of both events (the crossing of the Rhine by the barbarians and the rebellion of Constantine III in Britain) caused Stilicho to waver. For some time, his attentions had been focused on the east. For the rumours that had been circulating – that Stilicho had made a pact with Alaric – were apparently true. Plans were already well developed: the two men would soon be fighting side by side to wrest Illyricum from Constantinople's control, and deliver it to Rome, so giving Stilicho the potential for recruiting more Gothic troops, and Alaric the territory he wanted for his homeland.

But now, with Honorius' rule in Gaul threatened not only by the barbarians but also by a rival emperor, their plans had to be rapidly aborted. Abandoning Alaric, Stilicho raced to Rome, where Honorius and his court were in residence. Quickly, he persuaded them to send an army to Gaul led not by him, but by the Gothic general Sarus. Why Stilicho chose Sarus, when he himself had troops on stand-by and Alaric, too, was in battle-readiness, cannot now be known. Sarus had already fought with some distinction against the Gothic chieftain Radagaisus in 405/6. But, as subsequent events would show, he was decidedly unstable. In the end, his actions would help bring down not just Stilicho but Rome.

Meanwhile, events seemed to be moving faster than Stilicho could cope with. At home, his daughter Maria had died. For a ghastly few weeks, Stilicho was no longer Honorius' father-in-law. Only a hastily arranged marriage between Honorius and Maria's sister Thermantia restored the status quo.

Then Alaric began behaving contrary to plans. Left to his own devices, cast adrift after the aborted Illyrican campaign and now, presumably, no longer bankrolled by the eastern empire, he had by 408 crossed over to the province of Noricum, to the north-east of Italy. From there, he sent an envoy to Stilicho, demanding money for the expenses allegedly incurred in preparing for the expedition to Illyricum.

When news of Alaric's latest move reached Rome, the Senate voted overwhelmingly for war on Alaric, but Stilicho persuaded them against it. The campaign against the eastern empire, he argued, had been Honorius' idea, which had only been averted by the quick thinking of Stilicho's wife, Serena, so eager was she to maintain good relations between east and west. Even so, the pact made between the emperor and Alaric must be honoured. The money must be paid.

The Senate probably suspected that Stilicho's argument was disingenuous to say the least. Nonetheless, even as one of its number grumbled, 'this is not peace but voluntary enslavement', it voted to pay Alaric 4,000 pounds of gold. The episode marked a turning point: senators who had once supported Stilicho now felt intimidated by him; even Honorius could sense that things had changed. Falsely accused of plotting against his brother in the east – and no longer the boy he had been when Stilicho had first imposed himself as his guardian – the emperor began to distrust him more and more. A rift had opened up between them.

The first signs that all was not well at the palace appeared within days, when Honorius tried to insist on accompanying Stilicho on his journey from Rome to Ravenna. Stilicho did everything in his power to stop him, even getting Sarus (now back from his short and unsuccessful campaign against Constantine III) to frighten the emperor by staging a mini-mutiny at Ravenna. Curiously, however, Serena took Honorius' side. Keen to preserve her influence at court, it was in her interests to keep Honorius safe; and Ravenna, she felt, was the best place for him.

In the summer of 408, while making his imperial progress up the Flaminian Way en route to Ravenna, Honorius received confirmation of a rumour he had heard days earlier. Arcadius, his brother, the emperor of the east, was dead.

Suddenly, everything began to happen at once. Some of the army stationed in Italy mutinied. When order was restored, Stilicho condemned its leaders to death. But then Honorius countermanded Stilicho's orders and pardoned the condemned mutineers. The episode marked the start of a jostle for power, as general and emperor began to realize that one of them would have to go.

For both had ambitions in the east. Honorius immediately announced that he wanted to travel to Constantinople to offer his protection to the new eastern emperor, his seven-year-old nephew, Theodosius II. But he was opposed by Stilicho – who was determined to make the journey himself – desperate, it was said, to become the young boy's guardian. Think of the expense, Stilicho reasoned, of the security involved in an imperial journey east. Besides, this was no time for Honorius, the emperor, to leave Italy, when his western provinces were so wracked by upheaval, and Alaric, an 'untrustworthy barbarian'[65] remained close by. It would be much better to send Alaric immediately against Constantine III in Gaul, while Stilicho went as Honorius' envoy east to Constantinople. Meekly, Honorius acquiesced.

But inexplicably, nothing happened. It was as if Stilicho, so energetic all his life, was suddenly seized by lethargy. As the days dragged by, he neither communicated his commands to Alaric nor made preparations of any kind to set out for the east. Perhaps he was afraid to leave Italy, knowing that the tide had turned against him. Perhaps, for the same reason, he was loath to lose his ally, Alaric, to the conflict in Gaul. Perhaps he feared that Alaric would gain too much power if he were successful. As he weighed up what to do, he did nothing.

It was the moment that his enemies had been waiting for. The eunuch Olympius hated Stilicho, and now saw his chance. He started spreading rumours that Stilicho

> was planning an expedition to the east, where he was
> plotting to overthrow young Theodosius and to install his

own son, Eucherius, on the throne. As they travelled, Olympius would make such allegations to the emperor, whenever he had the chance. When they reached Ticinum, he paid a visit to the sick and wounded soldiers and (as the culmination of his sanctimonious hypocrisy) cast his spells among them.[66]

Had he wanted to, Olympius could have helped his cause further if he had pointed out that Stilicho had already paved the way for his son's elevation by engaging him to Honorius' sister, the young Galla Placidia.

Four days after his arrival at Ticinum, modern Pavia, near Milan, Olympius performed the first move in an elaborately staged *coup d'etat*. As Honorius prepared to address the army stationed there, prior to their setting out for Gaul to fight Constantine III, Olympius gave the signal. At once, the soldiers involved in the conspiracy seized and slaughtered four of their officers. As the violence spread, Honorius retreated into the palace, leaving his soldiers to run amok throughout the city. Members of the city council were hunted down and killed, and buildings were looted and ransacked. For a moment, Honorius showed extraordinary courage, when, dressed 'in a short tunic, and without even his crown, he showed himself in the middle of the city, where, with the greatest difficulty, he managed to calm the soldiers' rage.'[67] Eventually, and only after great loss of life, peace was restored to the streets of Ticinum.

As reports of events in the north reached Stilicho in Bologna, he called a hasty meeting of the leaders of the barbarian allies stationed there. Until they knew what had happened to Honorius, it was difficult to act. If the emperor were dead, they agreed that they would immediately launch an attack on the rebel Roman soldiers. If he were still alive, they would merely punish the instigators of the mutiny. But when news came that Honorius had been unharmed, Stilicho decided 'to return to Ravenna. Assessing the size of the Roman forces, and realizing that he could not trust Honorius, he thought it neither right nor safe to set barbarians against the Roman army.'[68]

**6.5** Interior of the church of Sant'Agata Maggiore in Ravenna. Built originally in the 5th century (some time after Stilicho's death), it is a good example of an early Christian basilica in Ravenna.

By now Stilicho must have known that support for him was slipping by the hour. Then as he lay sleeping, bivouacked by the road between Bologna and Ravenna, Sarus and his Goths slipped under cover of night into the Roman camp. Silently they crept up on Stilicho's Hunnic bodyguards. Expertly, efficiently, they slit their throats. When Stilicho awoke, it was as if to a nightmare. He managed to steal away and ride at a gallop to Ravenna, but Olympius had already sent orders on ahead to the garrison. Stilicho was a wanted man. The warrant was out for his arrest.

While his household and allies armed themselves and waited anxiously to see what would happen next, Stilicho took refuge in a church (*fig. 6.5*). Olympius' soldiers, led by Heraclian, came to the church at dawn on the next day (22 August 408). In the presence of Ravenna's bishop, Heraclian swore on oath that they had come only to arrest Stilicho, not to kill him. But when he had been led out, a messenger arrived with new instructions. Stilicho was to be put to death for crimes against the state.

When they heard the sentence, Stilicho's supporters tried to rescue him, but he had known for days that it was too late. He would go to his death nobly like an ancient Roman hero. As Heraclian raised his sword above his neck, Stilicho would not struggle…

Part 2 The storm clouds gather

PART 3

# *The sack of Rome*

# CHAPTER 7

# *Rome besieged*

*Rome's cheeks were sunken;*
*famine shrivelled her limbs.*
(Claudian, *War Against Gildo* 1.23–4)

Gold *solidus* of Galla
Placidia (c.388–450),
struck at Ravenna,
c.426–30 (see also
*fig.* 7.2).

Rome, early autumn 408... In the days
and weeks following Stilicho's murder, events
moved rapidly as tensions finally exploded in a bloody welter
of accusation and recrimination. With chilling efficiency, the
eunuch Olympius, now Honorius' chief advisor, orchestrated
a purge of anyone connected to the murdered general.

Determined to have public proof that Stilicho had been
plotting to overthrow Honorius, Olympius immediately ordered
the arrest of some of the administration's top officials. In an
attempt to elicit a confession, he had them brutally tortured in
front of the crowd at Ravenna. When coercion failed, he had
them clubbed to death.

Despite the lack of any evidence against them, Stilicho's
family overnight became *personae non gratae*. All official ties with
them were severed. Most prominent among them was Stilicho's
daughter, Thermantia, who was Honorius' wife. After hastily
divorcing her, Honorius sent Thermantia back to her mother,
Serena, in Rome.

More problematic was Stilicho's son, Eucherius, engaged to
the emperor's half-sister, Galla Placidia. As a male heir, he might
be expected to rally opposition, so could not be allowed to live.
Even as the boy's killers were tracking him down, the imperial
propaganda machine had swung into action, inventing lies and
smears. Stilicho, they claimed, had been planning to make
Eucherius emperor, which was why he had engaged the boy

to be married to Galla Placidia. Even worse, Eucherius had apparently secretly vowed that, once he became emperor, he would reinstate the worship of the pagan gods and persecute the Church.

The circumstances of the boy's killing are confused. The historian Zosimus, the only source, suggests that Eucherius first sought sanctuary in a church in Rome, where his life was spared. He may subsequently have escaped, because later Zosimus describes how two eunuch assassins found the boy and brought him back to Rome, where they executed him. The eunuchs were rewarded lavishly with high positions at court.

Meanwhile, the political map was being re-drawn. An imperial decree published in autumn 408 confiscated the property of all who had held office under Stilicho, while (crucially, as it would turn out) his brother-in-law, Bathanarius, was stripped of his post as commander of Africa. The choice of his successor was significant. It was none other than Heraclian, the man who had killed Stilicho.

Emboldened by these moves, the imperial troops went on the rampage. In an orgy of violence and destruction, they targeted the *foederati* – the barbarian soldiers who had formed the backbone of Stilicho's army – raping and massacring their wives and children and looting and destroying their homes. The result was all too predictable. The *foederati* vowed vengeance, and 30,000, as a man, changed allegiance – switching from the emperor to Alaric.

For Alaric was on the move again. By autumn negotiations with the court had broken down. The 4,000 pounds of gold that he had been promised – his price for helping Stilicho – had not been paid; and now that Stilicho was dead it clearly never would be. Moreover, the Goth's offer to withdraw his army far from Italy into Pannonia had been rebuffed. Treated with high-handed derision by the empire, his authority with his own people would soon be on the line. For Alaric, time and patience had run out. Late in the year, he sent urgent messengers to the Danube, to his sister's husband, Ataulf, pressing him to join them with his army as swiftly as possible. But he could not wait until Ataulf came. With winter fast approaching, he struck camp and led his people

**7.1** The Walls of Rome, just west of the Porta San Paolo (Porta Ostiensis), originally built by Aurelian (r. 270–5) and Probus (r. 276–82). Their height was almost doubled by Maxentius (r. 306–12) and they were again restored by Honorius in 403.

west again to Italy. But this time Alaric's goal was not the cities of the northern plains. This time his goal was Rome itself.

How the news of Alaric's advance was received at Ravenna is not recorded; how the court reacted is. It did nothing. Perhaps it was paralysed by fear, disbelief or indecision. Perhaps it hoped that the eastern empire would send urgently needed troops to help, particularly now that Stilicho – the cause of so many previous disputes – was dead. For, with the desertion of the *foederati*, the western army was seriously stretched and under strength. Perhaps the court had calculated that it simply could not win a battle against the Goth. And so Alaric was left to pass unchecked through the northern cities of Aquileia and Concordia, to Cremona and then south, as if, wrote Zosimus, he were on his way to a festival. If the court believed that Alaric's goal was Ravenna, they were soon proved wrong. Whether he intended to snub the court by ignoring the city as he marched on by, or whether he simply knew that he could not take it, Alaric pressed on. He sacked Rimini (Ariminum) and, using the Flaminian Way as if it were his own, marched south along the Adriatic coast,

Part 3 The sack of Rome

destroying various cities along the way, before following the ancient road across the Apennines to Rome (*fig.* 7.1).

With each report that arrived, Rome grew more fearful; with that fear suspicion swelled, and with suspicion came paranoia. In the face of Ravenna's failure to act, the Romans felt a sense of powerlessness. Yet it must be someone's fault, and they must have a scapegoat. In the absence of another, they accused Serena, Stilicho's widow still in Rome, of collaborating with the enemy. In late 408 a meeting of the Senate was convened, at which she was condemned to death. The vote was supported by the fifteen-year-old Galla Placidia, whom Serena had brought up as her own child, and who had once been betrothed to Serena's son, Eucherius.

Placidia had been privileged from birth. As a small child, she had been granted her own household – an enormous wealth, which made her unusually independent. On her father's death, she had become the ward of Stilicho, when she was given the official title, *Nobilissima Puella* ('The Most Noble Girl'). Coins struck in her name[69] depict a strikingly handsome woman (*fig.* 7.2). Stylized though they are, they show her wearing her hair under an elaborate diadem and gathered up from her shoulders to set off her lustrous pearls and silks. She exudes power and privilege, the epitome of a late Roman empress.

Now that Serena's star had fallen, it may be that Placidia could not wait to escape the older woman's scheming, which had almost forced her into young Eucherius' bed. Or perhaps she feared that her association with Serena would compromise her own position; or that the Senate would condemn her, too, if she did not openly support Honorius in every way she could. Possibly, also, she felt that, with Serena gone, and with her new-found independence, she could take on the older woman's role, perhaps in time becoming the most dominant woman at court. As it turned out, the role she was to play would be quite extraordinary.

**7.2** Gold *solidus* of Galla Placidia, who is shown being crowned with a diadem by the Hand of God. The reverse depicts Victory bearing the Christian Cross.

If the Senate believed that by garrotting Serena they could save Rome, they were wrong. By October 408, before the Roman people could even fully comprehend the situation facing them, the Goths had the city surrounded. Even worse, they took control of Portus at the mouth of the Tiber. Nothing could get out, and nothing could get in. The Goths had cut off the food supply (*fig. 7.3*).

For a city that depended for its very survival on a round-the-clock import of grain and oil, it was a nightmare scenario. Everyone knew that it would not be long before Rome starved. To conserve what supplies remained in the city's granaries and warehouses, the daily handout was immediately cut by half. Eventually it would be cut to a third. For, to the authorities in Rome, it was inconceivable that Ravenna would not swiftly send an army to lift the siege.

But as the days went by, it became increasingly clear that no such army was coming. The imperial court, through policy or inertia, had abandoned the Eternal City to its fate. And its fate was becoming increasingly unbearable. Despite the best endeavours of wealthy individuals, such as the family of the emperor Gratian, who shared their own supplies (received as part of their imperial pension) with the city poor, starvation soon struck Rome, and with it all the horrors that starvation brings.

**7.3** The Granaries of Epagathus and Epaphroditus in Ostia were built in the reign of Antoninus Pius (r. 138–61). 'The emperors rewarded Rome with Africa and Egypt to feed the sovereign people and Senate ... by means of summer-sped fleets ... to fill our granaries with corn.' (Claudian, *Gildo* I, 49–55)

Part 3 The sack of Rome

Before long, the situation was so dire that reports of cannibalism began to circulate. If Zosimus[70] could not quite bring himself to believe in their truth, others[71] could. Writing a few years later, Jerome could not resist a certain tabloid-style sensationalism when he observed how mothers were driven to eat their suckling children, 'so that the belly received again what a short time before it had given forth.'[72]

In the overcrowded and unsanitary city of Rome, disease soon followed famine. With immunity dangerously lowered by malnutrition, infection spread like wildfire through the crowded tenements and slums. And with no access to the cemeteries (Romans still buried their dead outside the city walls), the dangers to health were compounded by the accumulation of unburied corpses throughout the city. Even if there had been no famine, the stench would have been enough to render Rome uninhabitable.

Never in its imperial history, nor for centuries before, had Rome been brought so low. It was inevitable that there were those among the older pagan families who blamed Christianity for this unprecedented catastrophe. When the old gods were still honoured, Rome ruled the world. Now, less than twenty years after their worship had been banned, the city had been brought to the brink of destruction.

Some in Rome, led by the city prefect, took faith in the inspiring example of Narnia, a hill-town in the south of Tuscany, which, they claimed, had been saved from Alaric's advance by pagan sacrifices. When the Tuscan townspeople had invoked their ancestral pagan gods, their entreaties had been answered by a violent thunderstorm and lightning, which had driven off the Goths. Now Rome's city prefect, hoping similarly to call up the power of the ancient gods with pagan sacrifice, arranged a private meeting with Pope Innocent I.

Innocent was a master of *realpolitik*. He had been bishop of Rome for some seven years, during which time he had supported Honorius' efforts to clamp down on heresies and sects antithetical to the Catholic Church. But now, faced with the imminent ruination of Rome, he agreed to allow anything that

**7.4** Relief on the Arch of Galerius at Thessalonica, dedicated in 303 to celebrate Galerius' victories over the Persians in 298. A merciless persecutor of Christians, Galerius (r. 293–311) performs a pagan sacrifice with his retinue; it was the kind of sacrifice that the Romans declined to carry out 100 years later in 409.

might help save the city, including pagan sacrifices. However, in an astutely political move, he stipulated that such sacrifices should be carried out in private, not by the state. Even *in extremis*, the Christian Church would not give up its hard–won status as the empire's religion.

But the Pope's offer was not good enough for the pagan priests, who had envisaged reinstating an annual ceremony dating back to Rome's foundation, at which sacrifices were made to Capitoline Jupiter calling on him to honour his ancient promise to King Numa to protect Rome with his thunderbolts (*fig.* 7.4). But now, when the idea was mooted, none of the senators dared to participate in a pagan event, which would have had to be held openly in the Forum and on the Capitol. When they realized that the ceremony could not be held, the priests refused to perform any sacrifices whatsoever, and the whole idea was quietly dropped.

In the face of siege and famine, the Senate held a crisis meeting. In a decision that would set an important precedent, they voted that, if the emperor would not come to their aid, they must act independently and make their own terms with the besieging Goths.

For ambassadors, the Senate chose two of its leading colleagues – one of whom, Joannes, already had good relations with Alaric – and entrusted them to conduct negotiations as they saw fit. However, perhaps thinking more of the grandeur of Rome's history than of her present predicament, the ambassadors appear to have misjudged their tone. In a meeting that has become legendary, they began by telling Alaric that, although Rome was ready to make peace, she was equally well prepared for war, being well armed and well trained and having no fear of the Goths.

> When Alaric heard that all the citizens had been drilled in arms and were ready to fight, he laughed heartily at the ambassadors and said: 'The thicker the grass, the easier it is to cut.' But when they turned to a discussion of peace, he spoke in terms that seemed excessive even for a boastful barbarian. He said that he would not end the siege unless he got all the gold in the city; and all the silver too; not to mention any moveable property that there might be in Rome; and all the barbarian slaves. When one of the ambassadors asked, 'If you take all this, what will you leave for us?', Alaric replied, 'Your lives'.[73]

The ambassadors returned to Rome, ostensibly to put Alaric's terms to the Senate. But the Goth held all the cards, and there was never any real doubt that he would be given what he asked for. The only question that remained was how to quantify the city's wealth. In the end, agreement was reached. Rome would give Alaric 5,000 pounds in weight of gold (1,000 more than was 'owed' under the previous treaty with Stilicho), 30,000 pounds of silver, 4,000 silk tunics, 3,000 scarlet-dyed skins and 3,000 pounds of pepper (demonstrating the value and worth of this exotic spice imported from far-off India) (*fig. 7.5*).

It was a vast wealth, and one not easy to raise. For the imperial treasury was, of course, with Honorius in Ravenna, and anyway the agreement made between Alaric and Rome had been reached privately. Responsibility for ensuring payment lay with the Senate, and more specifically with a relatively junior member, Palladius, who was given the thankless task of calculating how much each senator should pay from his own estates. Palladius must have been canny in carrying out his duty for he was rewarded a year or so later with the post of proconsul of Africa.

**7.5** ABOVE and OPPOSITE A selection of finds from the Hoxne hoard, buried in Suffolk, England, in the early 5th century: a silver pepper pot in the form of an empress (detail opposite), a bracelet bearing the name Juliana, and a woman's gold body chain. The hoard also contained numerous silver spoons, pieces of jewellery and over 15,000 gold and silver coins.

But the senators were loath to part with their ancestral wealth (*fig. 7.6*). Some prevaricated. Others hastily buried their treasures in the ground. Perhaps Palladius turned a blind eye but, in any event, he soon found himself unable to amass the agreed amount by conventional means. Instead, he arranged to remove the precious metal facings decorating the statues of the pagan gods, which still adorned many of the temples and public spaces. When the metal proved insufficient, he melted down yet more figures, made of solid gold or silver.

For the pagans, it was the final straw. They bitterly lamented the destruction of a statue of

> Bravery, which the Romans call *Virtus*. When it was taken away, such bravery and virtue as the Romans possessed went with it — which is what everyone who knew about traditional religion practices had predicted.[74]

Many must have reflected that the rot, which had set in when the Altar of Victory was removed from the Senate House, had finally spread to destroy the entire fabric of Rome.

In the dying weeks of 408, while Palladius was busy with his irksome task, the Senate sent ambassadors north to Ravenna to inform Honorius of the measures they had been forced to take and the agreements they had made. In addition, Alaric authorized the ambassadors to offer terms of his own: if the emperor chose to ratify the treaty and seal it – by an exchange of aristocratic child hostages – then the Goths would not only make peace, but would join in an alliance to fight Rome's enemies. In days the word came back. Honorius agreed to the terms.

Alaric, always quick to trust the Romans' word, allowed a temporary, three-day lifting of the siege and withdrew the bulk of his forces to the relative charms of Tuscany. In part, the move was to allow the barbarian slaves to leave Rome and come over to his side. The many who did swelled his force to close on 40,000. Partly, too, his action was to give the people of Rome some respite. After all, Alaric did not want to antagonize his new-found allies any further.

The three-day window allowed the citizens of Rome to replenish their food supplies and (one imagines) bury their dead. It was a period of frantic activity. Throughout the siege, ships from the provinces had still arrived at Rome's harbours of Portus and Ostia, and the goods had been unloaded into the warehouses. Now, in the precious few days of respite, there was a constant flow of traffic both by river and by road as the authorities did their utmost to ensure that the city was restocked. Again, Alaric was scrupulous in ensuring that the terms of the treaty were adhered to by both sides. He was careful to make an example of some of his own men who disobeyed orders and attacked a convoy of Romans on their way back from Portus with provisions.

At the end of the three-day period, the siege was resumed. As before, the Senate daily expected word from Ravenna that Honorius had carried out his part of the bargain and sent the hostages to Alaric. But the only news that reached them was of celebrations in Ravenna to mark the emperor's eighth consulship.

With the city sliding once again into starvation, the Senate chose three of its members who were the most experienced in the arts of diplomacy to go back to Ravenna and find out what was happening. One of the three was Priscus Attalus, a man with an impeccable record of service. A close friend of the late senator Symmachus, he had experience of serving on diplomatic

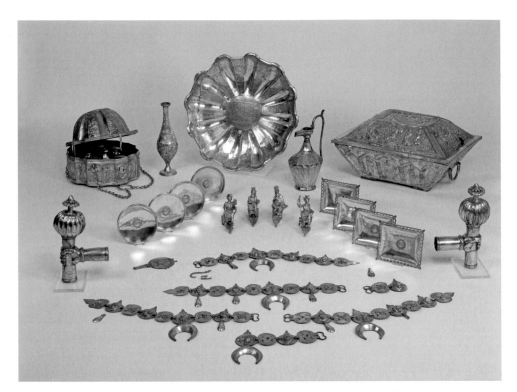

**7.6** This treasure, found in Rome on the Esquiline Hill, dates to the late 4th century. The casket was quite possibly a wedding present made for Secundus and Projecta, c.380. Probably she was a Christian, he a pagan. It is quite likely that such hoards were hidden in the years 408–10; some never to be recovered by their owners.

missions to Honorius, having previously been chosen by the Senate to negotiate over recruitment to the army.

Now, in the early days of January 409, as Attalus and his colleagues rode hard across the snowy Apennines on their journey north to Ravenna, they could have little idea of what awaited them. For Honorius himself felt under siege. As reports from all over Europe spelled out how his authority everywhere was crumbling, he must have felt his options dwindling by the day. More waves of barbarians were pouring west; the armies in the provinces were rebelling; Constantinople seemed a feckless ally; but, ideologically, alliance with the Goths was difficult to stomach. In the face of all this, the emperor of the west was becoming increasingly isolated. Increasingly he felt powerless to act.

# CHAPTER 8

# *Impotent emperors*

*He bragged that he would bring all the world under Roman rule, and other things besides that were even more excessive. Perhaps this is why the gods disdained him, and why, after a short while, they destroyed him.*

(Zosimus, *New History* VI.7.3)

Early January 409… Ravenna in winter can be rainy and raw, shrouded in a fog, which seeps and coils from the River Po, giving the city a sense of mystery and unreality. When Priscus Attalus and his fellow senators arrived at the imperial palace, they found that the mood of the court matched the weather.

Fed by his failure to find evidence against Stilicho, Olympius' personal vendetta had turned into an obsession. His spies were everywhere, watching, listening, and probing for any information that might lead to an arrest. At about this time, two brothers, both imperial notaries, were seized and brought to trial. Olympius had them tortured by the guard; but, like everyone else he had rounded up before them, they could not or would not give him the evidence he so feverishly desired.

In the light of the litany of disasters playing out around him, Olympius' monomania seems all the more remarkable. Only weeks before, an embassy had arrived from the usurper Constantine III, ostensibly begging Honorius' pardon for having elevated himself to the purple. Honorius, panicked by the presence of the Goths in Italy and reluctant to antagonize Constantine's well-armed, well-trained troops across the Alps in Gaul, had agreed to the pardon. But inexplicably, he had gone further. He had sent Constantine an imperial robe, a clear and

Silver medallion of Priscus Attalus (r. 409–10; 414–15), showing Roma enthroned (see also *fig.* 8.5).

unequivocal sign that he recognized him as a fellow emperor (*fig. 8.1*). The constitutional position was confused to say the least. For Attalus, it would provide a useful precedent.

But for now, such focus as remained at court rested on the Gothic question. In a meeting attended by both Honorius and Olympius, the Roman senators gave a vivid account of the suffering of Rome, the famine and the dead. They asked that the emperor ratify the treaty, which the Senate had made with Alaric, granting him the land he had asked for and exchanging hostages. Left to make his own decisions, Honorius might have acceded to their requests, but Olympius filibustered, introducing objections, muddying the waters. Perhaps he was distrustful of the treaty's terms, which seemed suspiciously moderate. Or perhaps it was more personal. Perhaps he could not stomach entering upon a treaty with someone who had previously been perceived to have a close association with his *bête noir*, Stilicho. Whatever Olympius' reasons, the meeting ended without agreement. In a misjudged bid to placate the senators, Honorius appointed one of them, Caecilianus, prefect of Rome. To Attalus, he passed a poisoned chalice – the post of *Comes Sacrarum Largitionum* (finance minister). Then he sent them home.

But before he did so, Honorius assembled five legions, crack troops from Dalmatia, under the command of a gung-ho battle-hardened general, who, inauspiciously, shared his name with the emperor defeated at Hadrianople – Valens. The troops were to accompany the senators to Rome and act as city garrison. Again, Honorius' thinking is hard to compute, but the suspicion is that, as so often, he or his advisors had seriously miscalculated, under-estimating both the strength of the Goths and the threat to Rome.

Alaric, of course, could not allow the Dalmatian troops to reach the beleaguered city. Even if the timing or terrain were against him, he would have to join battle no matter what the cost. But the Roman general Valens played straight into his hands. Scornful of the Goths, he led his troops along the obvious route, the Flaminian Way, familiar to Alaric from the year before. In the lonely mountain passes an ambush was almost too easy. Of the 6,000 Dalmatian soldiers who had set out, only 100 reached Rome. That

Valens and Attalus were among them suggests that they fled on horseback very early on.

In the Senate, Attalus' report of Honorius' behaviour and Alaric's ambush was met with incredulity. Quite justifiably, the senators felt aggrieved. They had honoured their part of the agreement with Alaric, collecting the bounty, which the Goth had demanded. But now that Honorius had refused to ratify the treaty, Alaric had intensified the siege, allowing no one in or out of the city without his express permission. Supplies were again running low and, unless something was done quickly, total starvation was not far off.

So they voted to send a second embassy to Honorius, probably led by Attalus, and certainly including Pope Innocent. While arrangements were being made, Attalus used his position as chief finance minister to nail his political colours to the mast, and purge his immediate office of anyone appointed by Olympius. This included Olympius' chief inquisitor, the curiously mild-mannered Heliocrates.

> He had been given the job of investigating property –
> confiscated because of its owners' association with Stilicho
> – and then of turning it over to the Treasury. But, as he
> was a fair man, and thought it sinful to take advantage of
> others' misfortunes, he was lax in his investigations and
> secretly advised many to hide what they could. So he was
> considered a miscreant and summoned to Ravenna to be
> punished for his kindness towards those in trouble. And,
> given the prevailing inhumanity, he would have been
> condemned to death, had he not taken sanctuary in a
> Christian church.[75]

Because of the blockade of Rome, permission for the embassy to leave the city had to be sought from Alaric, who sent a detachment of his own men to accompany it on the journey. Ostensibly for the embassy's protection, no doubt it also ensured

**8.1** Gold *solidus* of Constantine III (r. 407–11), struck at Trier in 408–11. The reverse shows the victorious emperor trampling a barbarian. Although Constantine did win some victories against barbarians, his campaigns were not as conclusive as the coin suggests.

that full and frank reports of what was agreed got back to Alaric. If Attalus hoped that the situation, which awaited him at Ravenna, would be conducive to rational discussion, he was badly mistaken. If anything, the chaos at court was greater than anything he could have imagined. News had just reached it that Alaric's brother-in-law, Ataulf, to whom he had sent for reinforcements in the previous autumn, had already crossed into Italy and was heading south.

Never for a moment does it seem that the court considered making any kind of peace. Instead, Honorius sent out frantic messages to all the garrisons in Italy to mobilize against the new invasion. Summoning Olympius, he gave the eunuch command of the imperial regiment of 300 Huns based at Ravenna, and sent him off to fight. To Olympius' credit, he did better than might have been expected. Finding Ataulf's army camped near Pisa, he attacked it in the night and (according to his own reports) killed 1,100 for the loss of only seventeen of his own men. But when dawn broke and Olympius saw the size of the Gothic army, he realized how heavily outnumbered he was, so turned and with his Huns fled back to Ravenna.

What happened next shows what a hotbed of intrigue the imperial court was (fig. 8.2). During the few days that Olympius had been away, his rival eunuchs had been hard at work, whispering in their master's ear that all the troubles of the empire were Olympius' fault. When he returned to Ravenna with his 283 surviving Huns, Olympius found the tables had already turned on him. He was immediately removed from office. All too aware of the fate that awaited those who fell from grace – a fate over which he himself had so often and so mercilessly presided – he escaped the city and fled in terror to Dalmatia.

The mood at Ravenna was clearly not conducive to pursuing peace talks with Alaric. Instead, Honorius kept Pope Innocent with him at court and once more sent Attalus back to Rome. But once more, before he did so, he gave him a new appointment – city prefect. Attalus would now be the most powerful man in Rome, second only to the emperor, with full authority over every aspect of the city's life.

This was not the only new appointment that Honorius made. Freed from the baleful presence of Olympius, he began to act in a way suggesting that, after all, he might possess some native wit. One of his most brilliant but controversial appointments was to the post of military commander in Dalmatia and the provinces extending northeast from the Alps. It was clear that the best man for the position was the barbarian-born general Generid. But there was a problem. Generid was a pagan and, under the law promulgated by Honorius after the assassination of Stilicho, only orthodox Christians were allowed to hold imperial office. In his interview with Generid, Honorius suggested that, in view of the pressing need, allowances could be made and rules bent to accommodate the appointment. But Generid, either as a matter of principle or because he knew his authority would be severely compromised if he accepted under such terms, held out for the law to be repealed. It was, and his command was marked by a return to old-fashioned army discipline, which made him a force to be reckoned with. Had he been in position only months before, Ataulf's entry into Italy might not have been so easy.

**8.2** Wall mosaic in the Basilica of San Vitale at Ravenna showing Justinian I (r. 527–65), bearing a golden dish. On the left, robed in white, two patricians are flanked by guards bearing a shield decorated with a Chi-Rho. The man on the right might be the eunuch general Narses. In front of him, Bishop Maximianus, bearing a cross, is flanked by another two priests.

Yet there were still those in Ravenna jostling to pick up the strings of power abandoned by the puppet-master Olympius. In a carefully orchestrated coup, the army garrison mutinied and occupied the harbour area. For a short while, Ravenna found itself in the same position as Rome, cut off from supplies and the sea, as the mutineers clamoured for Honorius to come in person to address their grievances. Honorius, of course, refused. According to Zosimus, he hid.

At that moment, a new *éminence grise,* Jovius, stepped up to the mark. A seasoned and wily career politician and a former ally of Stilicho, he had survived the purges of Olympius. Jovius was a patrician who knew well how to bend with the prevailing wind, having previously served as Alaric's representative in Epirus before becoming Honorius' praetorian prefect, essentially the head of the imperial civil service.

Now, he easily persuaded the terrified emperor to let him deal with the mutinous soldiers, who, as it quickly turned out, may have been hostile to Honorius but were suspiciously loyal to Jovius. His price – the arrest of some of his political enemies, who were subsequently killed en route to exile – was regarded, in the circumstances, as not altogether unreasonable.

The stage was now clear for Jovius to pursue what seems to have been his ultimate goal: ratification of the treaty with Alaric, a man with whom he had worked closely in Epirus and who considered him a friend. Acting now on Honorius' behalf, Jovius invited Alaric and Ataulf to Ravenna for peace talks. At last, an end to the years of turmoil seemed to be in sight. With the general Generid commanding Roman forces in Dalmatia, and Alaric no longer threatening Italy, the western empire could turn its attention to the usurper Constantine III in Gaul. In time, perhaps Honorius could even re-impose his rule throughout his empire, both east and west.

But, as invariably happened, the whole thing went disastrously wrong. To begin with, Alaric and Ataulf refused to go to Ravenna, preferring to meet on more neutral ground at Rimini. Perhaps, too, they felt that the talks would have more chance of success if Honorius were not present (for there was little chance that the fearful emperor would leave Ravenna). But if this were the case, it was, as it turned out, a serious miscalculation.

The meeting between Alaric and Jovius went well. Alaric put forward his demands for money and a homeland for his people. Jovius duly recorded the Goth's terms in a letter to Honorius, written in Alaric's presence, and then despatched by imperial courier to Ravenna. Had it been the only letter that he sent, things might still have turned out very differently. But it was not. For reasons we can only guess at, Jovius added to the diplomatic pouch a letter of his own, suggesting that it might be politic, not only to grant Alaric's demands, but also to appoint him *Magister Utriusque Militiae*: the post of five-star general that Stilicho had held and Alaric had always craved. Perhaps the move was part of Jovius' strategy to assimilate Alaric back under the command of Rome. But if so, it backfired spectacularly.

When the courier returned from Ravenna with Honorius' reply, he found Jovius waiting for him in Alaric's tent.[76] So supremely confident was he that Honorius would accede to all the conditions laid out that he ordered the seal to be broken and the letter read out in Alaric's presence. The first few paragraphs went as expected. Honorius granted Jovius permission to make whatever agreement he saw fit in terms of money and land. But, as the courier read on, Jovius realized too late that the imperial communiqué included Honorius' views – expressed in no uncertain terms – on Jovius' private suggestion that Alaric be made a general. Under no circumstance, the letter stated, would Honorius consider giving any sort of honour, military or otherwise, to Alaric or any of his family. He had just got rid of Stilicho. Why would he want another barbarian lording it in the halls of Ravenna? The meeting broke up in acrimonious confusion. Furious and humiliated, Alaric ordered the trumpet to be sounded for camp to be broken and his men to march back to Rome. Shame-faced and fearing for his own position, now that his misjudgement had resulted in a debacle of monumental proportions, Jovius scuttled back to Ravenna.

Once there, he immediately sought an audience with the emperor and assured him of his loyalty, swearing an oath never to make peace with Alaric, but rather to wage total war until the Goth had been defeated. To magnify the significance of his allegiance and demonstrate it as powerfully as possible, he swore the oath with his right hand laid on Honorius' head. He then made the other officials do the same, and set about sending for Hunnic troops from Thrace, and supplies of corn and cattle from Dalmatia in preparation for an all-out war.

Again, Jovius had miscalculated disastrously. In his rush to save his skin, he had overlooked what he knew about the Goth. Alaric was driven not by hostility to Rome but by a desire for a homeland – a desire so overwhelming that it was very likely that, given time to cool down, the volatile Goth would change his mind. And this is precisely what happened:

> But Alaric had second thoughts about his march on Rome and sent bishops as ambassadors to each of the cities, saying that they should appeal to the emperor not to let a city that had ruled over the greater part of the world for more than a thousand years be sacked by barbarians; nor to allow its splendid buildings to be burnt, but to make peace straightaway on equitable terms. For Alaric did not want high office or repute. Nor did he want those provinces that he had previously demanded as his homeland, but only the two Noricums, which lie at the furthest reaches of the Danube, for they are regularly under attack and pay little in the way of tax. In addition he would be content with however much corn the emperor saw fit to give him on an annual basis. Forget about the gold; instead there would be friendship and military alliance between Alaric and the Romans, who would together oppose all who took up arms and waged war against the emperor.[77]

As peace terms go, Alaric's were almost ludicrously fair. But the Gothic king had not taken into account the political constipation that was Ravenna. As far as the court was concerned, an oath was an oath, and an oath taken on an emperor's head was binding and could not be revoked. They had sworn collectively to wage war on Alaric, so wage war they would, no matter what the consequences. There was no room for manoeuvre. There was no going back.

Frustrated and angry, Alaric returned to Rome, his options dwindling, but with one final daring plan in mind. Even if Ravenna would not grant him what he wanted, Rome still might. But for Rome's writ to have any legitimacy, it must somehow use its power to trump that of Ravenna. The Roman Senate, which could still wield considerable constitutional and political power, must be persuaded, by force if necessary, to stage a *coup d'etat*.

At first, the Senate rebuffed Alaric's suggestions. But when the Goths turned up the pressure – seizing Portus and Ostia and threatening not only to cut off the food supply completely but also to burn the warehouses and distribute their stock among his men – the senators began to question whether they really owed Honorius anything. After all, he had lifted not a finger to help them in their troubles. Indeed, he seemed content to let Rome starve while he fattened up his flocks of pet hens in Ravenna (*fig. 8.3*). With the spectre of a slow and certain death staring them unflinchingly in the face, and encouraged perhaps by Attalus, who had seen at first-hand the state of inertia at the court, the senators invited Alaric into the city and the Senate House.

Writing at around this time, the intellectual Synesius[78] heaps scorn on the contemporary barbarian: like a chameleon, he sheds his animal skins and dons a toga to enter the Senate House and debate with the senators, only to change back again quickly, as the toga made him feel uncomfortable. Synesius could almost have been describing Alaric.

Swathed in a purple-trimmed toga, Alaric addressed the Roman Senate. As he did so, he was aware that he had come not only as Rome's conqueror but also as her kingmaker. For his intention now was nothing less than to appoint Honorius' successor, the next emperor of the west. And his shortlist of candidates was short indeed. It contained only one name – Priscus Attalus, prefect of Rome.

How long Attalus had coveted the imperial purple cannot be known. Perhaps his ambition had been fuelled in Ravenna

the year before, when he heard how readily Honorius had recognized the claims of Constantine III. Or perhaps his appointment as Rome's prefect had brought home to him that to wield power effectively, he must also have ultimate authority.

The scene in the Senate House on that day, 3 November 409, was as extraordinary as any witnessed in its history (*fig.* 8.4). But for once there was a mood of unanimity, perhaps even of optimism, as each faction felt that the decisions being made could potentially improve their situation beyond imagining and give them the power they felt was rightly theirs.

For the Senate, sidelined for so long and now apparently abandoned while the imperial court made its capital in cities far from Rome, here at last was an opportunity to regain something of its former prestige. True, it had been called upon a decade earlier to wield authority by Stilicho in his spat with the east. True, too, it still held the power of life and death over individuals like Serena. It may even have hoped that Honorius might one day actually move his court back to the ancient capital, as he had at times coyly flattered the Senate into believing that he would. But now here at last was a genuine chance that things would really change. Attalus was one of

Part 3 The sack of Rome

their own, an aristocrat who could represent their interests; his bailiwick was Rome; he understood the Senate and recognized its worth.

For Alaric, the situation offered a chance to gain the legitimacy he so craved, and with it the stability of an established homeland for his people. It could and has, of course, been argued that, by imposing Attalus as emperor, Alaric was simply setting up a puppet of his own in opposition to the puppet at Ravenna. But the way things played out in the months that followed suggest otherwise. Rather, decisions made by Attalus show clearly that he was able to act independently of his Gothic patron. Alaric, for his part, was simply trying to break the logjam of inaction, which was stifling any hope of progress, not only in Rome and Italy but also in the greater western empire.

For Attalus had vision and ambition, as his speech to the Senate on the next day would show. But first, invested as emperor and seated on the imperial throne, he raised his right hand in the traditional gesture that symbolized the speaker's legitimacy.[79] Then he announced his appointments to the chief offices of state. The running of the government was entrusted to members of the Senate, while control of the army naturally fell to the Goths. Alaric finally received the supreme military post he

**8.4** The Senate House (right) in the Roman Forum. The original, from the time of Julius Caesar (d. 44 BC), was rebuilt by Diocletian after a fire in 283. The Altar of Victory was removed in 384–5, leading to the great confrontation between Symmachus and Ambrose. It was here that many momentous decisions were made in the years leading up to the sack of Rome in 410.

craved (*Magister Utriusque Militium*), while Ataulf took charge of the household cavalry.[80] In a move that demonstrated how his administration needed to embrace all men of talent, Attalus appointed as one of Alaric's lieutenants, Valens, whose 6,000 Dalmatians had been massacred by the Goths only weeks before.

According to some, who wished to present Attalus' regime as doomed from the start, his short journey to the imperial palace was accompanied by unfavourable omens;[81] and his pagan detractors went on to criticize his address to the Senate as bombastic and arrogant, an act of hubris that could not but attract the anger of the gods. But his supporters praised his speech as brilliantly constructed, promising 'to protect the Senate's traditional rights and to make Egypt and all the eastern empire subject to the people of Italy'.[82] In other words, Attalus' ambition was not only to restore the power of Rome but, like that of Stilicho before him, to reunite the empire under one command.

He was, after all, from the east himself and his experience straddled not only both halves of the empire, but both religious traditions, too. Born into a wealthy family in Ionia (western Turkey), he had been brought up as a pagan. It was only as emperor that he had been baptized – like Alaric and Constantine I before him – by an Arian bishop. The coins struck hurriedly in the weeks that followed his appointment suggest that he was casting himself firmly in the imperial mould: although stylized, his portrait shows a big-boned face, with a strong jaw and large eyes; full hair combed forward in the ancient manner, the imperial diadem encircling his head (*fig.* 8.5).

On the day of Attalus' accession, Rome rejoiced.[83] The gates were opened wide, and people poured out, jostling down the Ostian Way to the warehouses of Portus, delighting that the time of famine lay behind them. It would not be many months before they realized, too late, how wrong they were.

**8.5** Silver medallion of Priscus Attalus, struck at Rome, c.409, and weighing four ounces. Such large silver items were probably made as presentation pieces, but it is also possible that there was a shortage of gold after Alaric's demands had been met in 409. The reverse shows Roma enthroned and bearing Victory, with an inscription proclaiming 'Eternal and Invincible Rome'.

# CHAPTER 9

# *Barbarian puppets*

*Pretium inpone carni humanae!*
(Put a price on human flesh!)

(Chanted by the crowd in the Circus Maximus
during the famine of the summer of 410.)

As the crowds surged out to the warehouses
of Portus, it must have seemed clear – at least to the
wiser heads in Rome – that it was on these very warehouses that
the fate of the city would ultimately depend. (*fig.* 9.1). It was
certainly clear to Alaric.

With Rome dependent on the constant import of corn and
oil from Africa, it was essential that the source of such vital
commodities should lie in Roman hands. But they did not.
Instead, controlling the supply of food from Africa was

Copper alloy
*Contorniate,* 4th
century, showing the
Circus Maximus (see
also *figs* 1.6 and 9.5).

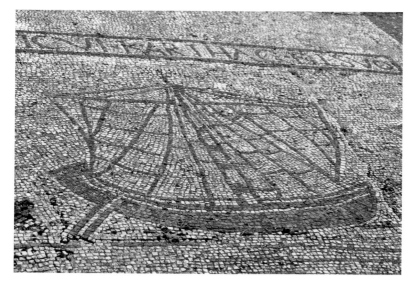

**9.1** Mosaic from
outside an office in
Corporation Square
at Ostia, 2nd–3rd
century. The
inscription tells
us that the office
belonged to shipping
agents trading with
Carthage (Karthag
on the mosaic). The
image of the ship
under sail makes the
agents' trade clear
to the visitor.

**9.2** A view of part of the Roman city of Dougga in modern Africa, showing fertile lands in the hinterland. Africa became the main bread-basket of Rome after Constantinople took over the supply of grain from Egypt. 'Africa remained our only hope and even she could scarcely feed us'. (Claudian, *Gildo* I, 62–3)

Honorius' appointee, the ruthless Heraclian (*fig.* 9.2). Alaric moved quickly to try to persuade Attalus and the Senate that Heraclian should be disposed of.

After all, time was of the essence. Not only must there be no break in the flow of goods to Portus but, if the new regime at Rome acted swiftly enough, it might be able to trick Heraclian into relinquishing power before he had even heard that Attalus had usurped the imperial throne. One stratagem, inspired by Johannes, a minister in the new government, involved faking an imperial letter with a counterfeit seal – supposedly from Honorius – which relieved Heraclian of his command.

Alaric himself was less than impressed by the plan. Instead, he urged that a Gothic army be sent directly to Carthage to overthrow Heraclian and thereby ensure once and for all the uninterrupted flow of food to Rome.

Attalus took the advice of neither man. Instead, he sent an envoy, Constans, to Carthage, charged with negotiating with Heraclian and persuading him to continue trading with the rebel emperor, Attalus, in Rome. His motives are obscure to say the least. It may be that he was loath to start his new reign by shedding the blood of a fellow Roman, especially at the hands of a barbarian assassin. It may even be that he did not want the

Goths to gain control of the grain supply. But the ancient sources suggest another more bizarre reason: Attalus had been persuaded by the seers that Carthage and Africa would fall to him without a fight.

It is easy, from a modern vantage point, to dismiss such accounts as the exaggerated or sensationalist propaganda of Roman historians who were hostile to Attalus and his regime. But for a man like Attalus, brought up as a pagan and living in extreme and unpredictable conditions, the advice of seers might well have seemed as good as any, especially when it coincided with what might have been his own political instinct. Moreover, he must have known that the legitimacy of his claims would be enhanced by a diplomatic solution. Certainly, he was able to persuade the Senate (perhaps still coming to terms with the possibilities of its new-found power) to rubber-stamp his decision.

While Constans was sailing south in his galley to Carthage, Alaric and Attalus marched north at the head of a huge army of Romans and barbarians. When they reached Rimini, they encountered a high-powered delegation sent by Honorius. Led by the chief minister Jovius, its proposals were predictable in the extreme: in return for peace, Honorius was willing to recognize Attalus as co-emperor. It was, of course, what Attalus had expected all along; but with Constantine III in Gaul already openly sporting the imperial purple robe that Honorius had sent him the year before, there would now be potentially three legitimate emperors simultaneously wielding power in the west. The imperial office was becoming distinctly crowded.

Unlike Constantine, Attalus was not prepared to accept Honorius' terms. He knew that three emperors would be two too many: a recipe for a weak and divided empire. Besides, his rapidly crystallizing vision of world domination could not accommodate any colleagues. Instead, Attalus sent Jovius back with an offer that he felt Honorius could not refuse. If Honorius abdicated, he would not be harmed in any way, but would be allowed to live with the trappings of an emperor on an island or any other place of his own choosing.

But just as earlier that year – when he had acted as go-between for Alaric and Honorius – Jovius could not resist amending the treaty. When he reported the terms to the court, Jovius included an intriguing clause of his own: before being exiled, Honorius should be disfigured. The nature of the proposed disfigurement was redolent with symbolism. The contemporary Church historian Philostorgius[84] reported that Honorius was to have his 'extremities' cut off. Subsequently, the eighth-century scholar Photius[85] was more explicit: Honorius was to be mutilated in one limb. The exact limb, it has recently and persuasively been argued,[86] was his right hand, the fingers of which, were usually extended while the emperor spoke, in a gesture symbolizing his legitimacy (see *figs* 3.4, 5.5 and 7.5).[87]

Attalus was shocked when he heard of Jovius' addition to his terms, and rebuked him, 'saying that it was not customary to mutilate an emperor who had willingly resigned his office'.[88] But the damage had been done. Honorius hesitated, and in his hesitation lay salvation.

For some time, Honorius had been contemplating flight. A fleet of warships lay at anchor in Ravenna's harbour waiting for the order to convey him east to Constantinople and asylum with his nephew, the nine-year-old emperor Theodosius II. Now the final hasty preparations were afoot to spirit him away. But at the very last moment, as so often in this story, the unexpected happened. Months before, years even, the court at Constantinople had promised to send an army to support the west. Now, under cover of night, with their oars muffled and silent, a small armada of black ships slid into the port at Ravenna. On board were 4,000 fresh and well-armed troops. The eastern army had arrived. Hope had returned to Honorius.

Yet it was a slender hope. To those involved, Honorius' position must have appeared precarious indeed. To the consummate survivor Jovius, the outcome already seemed sufficiently certain for him to abandon Honorius' camp and go over to Attalus, who rewarded him with a post in his government. In the toxic fishpond of Ravenna, the eunuch Eusebius rose up to take Jovius' place. But it would not be many months before, by public decree and in the presence of Honorius, Eusebius was beaten to death with rods.

Then, in the midst of all the turmoil, news reached Ravenna from Africa. For Honorius it was encouraging in the extreme. For Attalus and Alaric it spelled potential disaster.

The diplomatic mission to Africa had failed horribly. Constans, its leader, had been killed. Alerted to the situation in Italy, Heraclian, the commander, had put the province on a war footing, setting up garrisons in all the ports and stationing guards on lookout duty all along the coast. But worst of all, Heraclian had placed an embargo on any merchant ships bound for Rome (*fig.* 9.3). The food supply had been cut off.

Leaving Alaric camped outside Ravenna, Attalus hastily returned to Rome taking Jovius with him. In the city, the effects of the embargo could be clearly seen in the hollow eyes and emaciated figures of its already exhausted inhabitants. At a hastily convened meeting of the Senate, the emergency was hotly debated.

Many, including Jovius, urged that a Gothic army should be sent to Africa. Only such a force, they argued, would be able to fight its way ashore and have any chance of toppling the government in Carthage. But Attalus overruled them. Adamant that Rome should not be beholden to barbarians, and furious that the Senate was contradicting his own wishes, he issued orders that a Roman army should sail for Africa equipped with whatever money could still be found.

When Alaric heard of it, he was incandescent with rage. It seemed as if Attalus was intentionally wrecking any chance of success. Feeling increasingly helpless in the face of such incompetence, and beginning to suspect that a deliberate campaign of sabotage was being waged by some of Attalus'

**9.3** This relief, found in Carthage, is thought to show an African sailing a two-masted *corbita*, around 200. 'I saw rivalry between the grain ships and everywhere I looked I saw the African and Egyptian fleets competing.' (Claudian, *Gildo* I, 58–9)

**9.4** The Roman walls of Ravenna. Honorius carried out extensive work on the walls in the early 5th century, but later Roman and Gothic leaders also strengthened them in the century following. The walls proved strong enough to thwart Alaric in 410.

lieutenants, Alaric's wrath fell on Valens, so recently Honorius' man, but now commanding Attalus' cavalry. A summary court-martial was held. Valens, convicted of treason, was executed.

Yet it was Alaric who had put Attalus on the throne. And, for the moment at least, the Goth had to live with the situation he had created and make the best of it. As soon as the expected news arrived – that Attalus' task force in Africa had been defeated – Alaric switched strategy. Taking Jovius' advice, he lifted the siege of Ravenna, which, in any case, seemed impregnable, protected as it was by the marshes and the fresh reinforcements from the east (*fig.* 9.4). Instead, he turned his attention to the cities of Aemelia and Liguria. After securing their allegiance to the new emperor (by force if necessary), he gathered from them as many resources, food, funds and men, as possible.

The battle for the western empire had moved full square to Italy. But now it was a battle that Honorius sensed he could win. If, in order to preserve the heart of the empire, it was necessary to sacrifice lands far off across the seas, then the sacrifice would be worth making. In reality he had no choice. Britain had rebelled already. Much of Germany and Gaul was lost, while in the rest of Gaul and Spain power lay in the hands of Constantine III. So let Constantine face all the problems of the far west. It had elected him, after all.

Part 3 The sack of Rome

Instead, Honorius focused on regaining his power base with the armies nearer home. With the help of Heraclian in Carthage, who was for now at least awash with surplus money and food, the emperor lavished gifts on the armies and bought their support. To the soldiers, the contrast – between the bountiful Honorius and the hapless Attalus, presiding over his starving city – could not have been greater.

For the stories coming out of Rome were horrendous. Conditions were almost unimaginable. Food had run out. In the intensifying heat of the approaching summer, people were scraping in the dust for anything that might be found to eat. Not surprisingly, the mood of the citizens was turning increasingly ugly. There were rumours of people grinding acorns to make a gritty flour for bread; of merchants profiteering by hoarding what few supplies they had; and, once again, there were rumours of cannibalism. A tale was even circulating of how a starving throng had packed into the Circus Maximus (scene of Honorius' balletic mock battle only six years earlier), demanding that cannibalism be legitimized. A fevered chant had resonated round the marble benches: 'Put a price on human flesh!' (*fig. 9.5*).

**9.5** The original Circus Maximus, also shown on the inset medal, dates back to Republican times. Used for chariot races, athletic events, animal hunts and even mock naval battles, the stadium could hold around 385,000 spectators at its peak. It was also used for imperial displays, with emperors presiding from a box (pulvinar) just below the palace on the Palatine Hill (see also *fig. 1.6*).

The Senate met again. Again the case was made to send a Gothic army out to Africa. Again the motion met with almost unanimous support. Again Attalus opposed it. But this time, Alaric had a plan, and one for which he believed he had all the pieces already in place.

There could be no doubt that Attalus was a liability. It had been clear to everyone for months. It was as if God Himself was working to thwart any chances he might have of success. No one felt safe, not even the chameleon Jovius. Certain that Attalus, once secure, would gladly ditch his Gothic ally, Jovius had missed no opportunity to point out his shortcomings to Alaric. But Alaric needed no convincing. Going behind Attalus' back, he had entered into negotiations with Honorius. And now he had received imperial assurances of peace, but on one condition – as would soon become clear. Persuading Attalus to accompany him, Alaric set out for the last time to Ravenna. In his train, as a potential hostage, was Honorius' half-sister Galla Placidia.

On the plain before Ravenna, the two sides met to seal the treaty. But first, a sacrifice had to be made – the sacrifice of Attalus' power. Bewildered, Attalus could not resist as Alaric's men closed in and stripped him of his diadem and purple silks, which they folded neatly and conveyed, as had been agreed, to Honorius. Humiliated but still free, Attalus himself remained in the Gothic camp, where he realized he would be safer than in Honorius' court. Nevertheless, the one condition on which Honorius had insisted had been met: Attalus had been overthrown. The last impediment to peace was gone. The treaty between Alaric and Honorius could now be signed.

But it was not only in the Roman camp that personal vendettas and ambitions boiled. Among the Goths, too, bitter feuds seethed. Sarus the Goth, who had once served Stilicho before betraying him (see pp. 86–90), and who had, for a long time, nursed a grudge against Alaric, had recently arrived in Ravenna. Sarus, it seems,[89] had stood for leadership of the Goths at the time when Alaric had been appointed. Passed over and resentful, Sarus had harboured a growing hatred of Alaric ever since. Now he had found a way into Honorius' palace, where he had been treated courteously, with the respect that he felt was his due. Even if Honorius and Alaric were now allies, the presence of Sarus could throw their delicate *entente* into jeopardy. Besides, Sarus wanted Alaric to fail. And now he had found the perfect opportunity for his revenge.

As preparations for signing the treaty were reaching their conclusion, Sarus led his 300-strong band of Goths out of Ravenna and launched an attack on Alaric's camp. Despite his relatively small force, Sarus had the advantage of surprise and not a few of Alaric's men were killed. But, for Sarus, the attack was successful in a more significant way. Alaric, edgy and volatile, immediately suspected foul play on Honorius' part. Without waiting to find out the truth, he gave the order for his army to strike camp. As the barbarian trumpets bayed around the plain and echoed from the walls of Ravenna, his men hastily loaded their gear back on their wagons and turned their horses' heads for Rome.

Alaric's patience had run out. He had no more options left. Angry and humiliated and believing that he had been double-crossed, he now knew that his dream of a Gothic homeland had been lost for ever, and with it, potentially, his own credibility as his people's king. There was only one course left. To assuage his battered pride and teach his 'civilized' tormentors what barbarians could do, he would unleash his wrath on the city, which for centuries had symbolized the empire's certainty, its smug superiority. He would expose its weakness and duplicity. He would sack Rome.

# CHAPTER 10

# *Rome taken*

*Who could describe the horror of that night, and all its carnage? What tears are equal to such suffering? An ancient city, for so many years a queen, now falls in ruin, while throughout its streets lie countless corpses, motionless and still… death in ten thousand forms.*

(St Jerome, quoting Virgil's *Aeneid* II, 361ff. )

Gilt Chi-Rho detail on a silver plaque from the Water Newton hoard, Cambridgeshire, c.4th century (see also *fig. 10.3*).

No one knows who opened Rome's gates to Alaric and his Goths on 24 August 410.[90] Sources are confused, but all agree that *someone* let the barbarians in. The Goths had little skill and no track record in capturing cities by siege. But at Rome they had no need for siege engines. At Rome it was different. They already had their own sympathizers on the inside.

To contemporary writers, steeped in classical mythology, the attack naturally evoked memories of another, more distant catastrophe – the legendary siege of Troy.[91] Inevitably, the ghost of the Trojan Horse stalked many accounts of the barbarian siege of Rome.

One historian, Procopius,[92] gives two versions. In the first, clearly influenced by the story of Troy, he tells how Alaric sent into the city a crack team of 300 young men, disguised as slaves – gifts for particularly susceptible senators. Once these troops were in place within the city, Alaric made a great show of preparing to raise the siege, lulling the Romans into a false sense of security; leading them to hope that the Goths were about to leave. But, Procopius continues,

on the appointed day, Alaric armed all his army for the attack and kept them in a state of high alert very close to the Salarian Gate (*fig.* 10.1). It so happened that this is where he had made his camp at the beginning of the siege. At the agreed time, the young men all gathered at the gate and suddenly attacked the guards and killed them. Then they opened the gate and received Alaric and his army into the city.

Procopius' second version of events puts the blame on Proba, the fabulously rich matriarch of the Anicii family, whose marbles were a byword for Rome's luxury. He writes that she

was moved to pity for the Romans who were starving and suffering so many other hardships – for already they were even eating human flesh. So, seeing that all hope had left them, and the river and the port were both in enemy hands, she ordered her servants to open the gates at night.

**10.1** The Porta San Paolo is one of several surviving gates in the walls of Rome. The main structure dates to the reign of Aurelian (r. 270–5), but the façade was rebuilt by Honorius in c.403. The gate gave access to the Ostian Way, which ran to Rome's ports. It probably saw much action in the events of 408–10. The Salarian Gate, through which Alaric's army gained access in 410, has not survived.

**10.2** The Mausoleum of Hadrian housed the cremated remains of Hadrian (r. 117–38) and his successors. Along with the Mausoleum of Augustus, it became a major focus of Alaric's looting in 410, when the ashes of the emperors were scattered.

Whoever was responsible, the outcome was the same. The Goths were in Rome. The city was at their mercy.

From the Salarian Gate, Alaric's men fanned out through the city. They had their orders and their objectives. Wholesale massacre and destruction would not be tolerated. Instead, the Goths would target iconic buildings, whose significance resonated deep in the Roman psyche.

Just inside the Salarian Gate lay the Gardens of Sallust, a palace complex built centuries before and funded by extortion in the provinces. Now rich in gold and jewels, they were soon pillaged. Everything that could be moved was looted, leaving only marble statuary behind – wounded Niobids and dying Gauls. Then the palaces were torched. More than a hundred years later, Procopius would shudder at the blackened ruins of their once opulently frescoed walls.

But more symbolic of the might of Rome were the mausoleums of the emperors Augustus and Hadrian (*fig.* 10.2). Deliberately singled out, they were quickly stripped and ransacked; the ashes of imperial dynasties, revered by generations, were scattered to the wind. It was an intentional and provocative act of desecration striking at the core of Rome's identity. To underline the point, the buildings themselves were left intact, but impotent and exorcised of all their ancient majesty and mystery.

The Church historian Orosius, writing only a few years later, gives some idea of the drama and confusion of the sack.[93] Alaric had issued a proclamation to his men – perhaps, too, to the citizens of Rome – that any who took refuge in chapels or churches, and especially in the Basilicas of St Peter and St Paul, should be unharmed. Many must have chosen to seek sanctuary here. The poor, especially, with nothing but their lives to lose, abandoned their tenements, so vulnerable to fire, and streamed through the night-time streets across the Tiber to the Vatican.

But others, perhaps too old or frightened, perhaps hoping to protect their homes and possessions, stayed put. Much of Orosius' account is taken up with describing one such, an elderly 'virgin of God', perhaps a nun, whose fate for him (and, indeed, for Gibbon[94]) encapsulates the greater sack of Rome.

He tells how one of the Goths, a 'powerful man and a Christian', entered her house. It belonged to the Church, so its occupants, if not its contents, were (in theory) safe. According to Orosius, he was polite, but demanded that the nun hand over any valuables she might possess. 'Resolute in her faith', the nun obliged. There was in her house, she said, a great deal of treasure, which she would bring out to him; and she laid out a collection of gold and silver vessels, the like of which the Goth had never seen (*fig.* 10.3). But, just as he was congratulating himself on his

**10.3** The oldest surviving set of Christian silverware from anywhere in the Roman Empire, the Water Newton treasure was hidden in the 4th century in Cambridgeshire. It contains a chalice, mixing bowls and a dish for bread or alms. Although it is a rich find, it must have palled by comparison with the silver plate owned by the major churches of Rome (see also detail, p. 124).

good fortune, the nun added: 'These are the sacred vessels of the Apostle Peter. Take them if you dare. You will be judged by what you do. Because I cannot defend them, I dare not keep them.' Impressed and no doubt somewhat taken aback by her portentous words, the Goth sent a messenger to Alaric to ask him what to do. Word came back that all the vessels should immediately be taken to St Peter's, along with the nun and any other Christians who might wish to join her. So began what must be one of the most unusual episodes of any sack in history.

The holy woman's house lay on the outskirts of Rome – far from St Peter's and the Vatican – so she, her fellow Christians and St. Peter's plate were given a special guard of honour by the Goths. Protected by a bristling wall of Gothic swords, the procession snaked through the streets of Rome, the treasure distributed among captors and captives alike, and raised high above their heads. At some point one of the Christians began to sing a hymn, which was soon taken up not only by the Romans, but by the Goths as well. Gradually, more and more people were attracted to the singing. Soon they poured out from their hiding places to join what had become a carnival. Some were true Christians, others just survivors who thought it politic for the moment to espouse the faith. The more Romans who joined the procession, the more avidly the Goths surrounded and protected them.

Orosius was a Christian with an agenda – to show how merciful Christians can be, even while sacking a city. Indeed, if the other predominantly Christian sources are to be believed, similarly miraculous events were taking place all over Rome. A Church historian recounts how a beautiful Roman woman vehemently fought off a passionate young soldier, who finally gave up in disbelief:

one young soldier in Alaric's army, enflamed by a particularly beautiful woman, wanted to drag her off and rape her. But she fought him off with all her power and did everything she could to resist, until he drew his sword and threatened to kill her. Yet, because of the lust he felt, he spared her, merely scratching her neck. When the wound bled freely, she offered her neck willingly to the sword, declaring that she would rather die a chaste woman, after a life lived virtuously with her husband, than survive to be raped by another man. The barbarian persisted, making ever more terrifying threats, but achieved nothing. At last, amazed at her chastity, he led her to the Basilica of St Peter the Apostle. There he handed her over to the guards, along with six gold coins, which he ordered them to keep safe for her husband [*fig.* 10.4].⁹⁵

**10.4** Glass medallion with an image of a man and woman in gold, probably found in the Catacombs at Rome, 4th century. The couple is shown being crowned by Christ, encircled with the inscription 'May you live [long] sweet soul'. Originally, the medallion probably decorated the base of a bowl, made as a wedding present.

But even devoutly Christian writers could not completely hide the true nature of the sack. For, although Alaric had ordered restraint, he was not universally obeyed. As they rampaged through the city, some of the Goths reached Marcella's Aventine palace – the monastic community that she had lovingly built up over many years. It was an impressive building. The Goths believed it was a rich one; so they broke down its doors and burst in. Writing later to Marcella's confidante, Principia, Jerome reminds her of the horrors of what happened next.

They say that, when the soldiers burst into her house, she received them with equanimity. When asked for her gold and hidden treasure, she pointed to her old worn tunic as a sign of her poverty. But they did not believe that she had really chosen the path of poverty. They say that, even when she was being beaten with clubs and whips, she felt

130        Part 3 The sack of Rome

no pain, but lay face down before them; and begged through her tears that you, Principia, might not be taken from her; nor that your youth might mean you would suffer what her old age meant that she had no need to fear. Christ softened their hard hearts and, amidst those bloodstained swords, Piety found a place. The barbarians escorted both you and Marcella to the Basilica of the Blessed Paul, that it might be your place of refuge, or your tomb.[96]

**10.5** *Romans Fending off the Goths,* etching by Johan Winckelmann, Germany, 1782. This scene was engraved at the time that Edward Gibbon was writing his *Decline and Fall of the Roman Empire* (1776–88).

A few days later, Marcella died of her injuries, in the arms of her pupil, Principia. Nor was Marcella alone. St Augustine tries valiantly to play down the extent of the slaughter in Rome, because he wants to suggest that (being Christian) the Goths were generally clement. But even he cannot completely sanitize his account.[97]

He writes of Romans (including Christians) being put to death in 'a hideous variety of cruel ways', of corpses left unburied in the streets, of slaughter, plunder, burning, misery, of citizens enslaved. And he writes of indiscriminate rape. Meanwhile, Jerome, in his correspondence with Demetrias, another young woman who had managed to escape the city, encapsulates the bleak reality: 'Rome, once the capital of the world, is now the grave of Roman people.'[98]

It is clearly wrong, then, to suggest that in some way the Goths were simply going through the motions of sacking Rome, doing the minimum of damage because, in fact, they would rather have done no damage at all. Frustration with the Roman Empire and the way it had treated them had been building up over many years. Now it was payback time (*fig.* 10.5).

These were, after all, men used to causing devastation. Their behaviour in Greece, albeit fourteen years earlier, shows what they were capable of.[99] As Gibbon comments:

Many thousand warriors, more especially of the Huns who served under the standard of Alaric, were strangers to the name, or at least to the faith, of Christ, and we may suspect, without any breach of charity or candour, that in the hour of savage licence, when every passion was inflamed and every restraint was removed, the precepts of the Gospel seldom influenced the behaviour of the Gothic Christians.'

It is likely that the chaos of the moment was an opportunity, too, for the settling of private scores among the inhabitants of Rome themselves. Gibbon goes on to write of how 'the private revenge of forty thousand slaves was exercised without pity or remorse; and the ignominious lashes that they had formerly received were washed away in the blood of the guilty or obnoxious families.'[100]

Those who could fled. Proba and her family, snatching what valuables they could, escaped by sea to the island of Igilium off the Etruscan coast, from where they watched the smoke pall rising over the burning city, almost 100 km away. Some years later the poet Rutilius, sailing past the island on his journey home to Gaul, remembered how it had 'welcomed many fugitives from the devastated city'.[101]

Meanwhile, there were those in Rome who were taking the chance to cash in on the general misfortune for their own private gain. The chroniclers tell of Roman citizens taken prisoner to be released only after ransom had been paid by relatives or well wishers; of others who were enslaved; of still others, from among the debutantes of Rome, who were trafficked as brides and sold to the highest bidder.

This last detail was reported by an outraged Jerome, who points out the irony of the situation. For, according to him, the prime villain in this trafficking scandal turned out to have been Heraclian, the commander of Africa, who had helped Honorius the year before by cutting off the corn supply to Rome. In a (more than slightly sensationalist) passage in his letter to Demetrias, Jerome writes:

> For she fell into the clutches of a man (Heraclian) whom I do not know whether to describe as more grasping or more cruel. To him nothing was sweeter than wine or

money. He claimed to serve the meekest emperor (Honorius), while being himself the cruellest of all tyrants… '*From mothers' arms he snatched their daughters though betrothed,*'[102] and sold noble girls in marriage to Syrian businessmen – the most grasping of any in the human race.[103]

Jerome adds that many of Heraclian's victims had their freedom bought for them by none other than Proba, who by now had made the perilous crossing from Igilium to Africa.

It was a time of unspeakable terror. To many it must have seemed as if the Day of Judgement was truly at hand. Orosius tells of an apocalyptic storm, in which 'the most famous places in the city, spared by the enemy, were destroyed by thunderbolts'.[104] Needless to say, he saw the thunderstorm as evidence that the hand of God lay behind the entire sack.

Herein lies the problem both for the Church Fathers and, as a consequence, for future generations. If God sanctioned the capture of Rome, and the Christian Goths were therefore doing His Will, then, as agents of God, their behaviour must be judged to have been in accordance with God's laws. For this reason, many of the Fathers play down the horrors of the sack while highlighting isolated incidents of clemency as representative of the wider picture. It required much spiritual and intellectual sophistry in order to reconcile the ghastly reality with the Christian ideal. But there would be time for such spiritual agonizing later. For now the brute realities still being faced were uppermost, causing crises of faith in both religion and the imperial dream.

Then, three days after they had entered Rome, the Goths left the city. They had done what they had come to do. They had made their point. Besides, there was no reason to stay, but every incentive to leave. The palaces were ransacked, emptied of everything that could be moved; marble floors littered with smashed shards and broken statuary; silks torn and hanging listlessly from empty walls and windows. In parts of Rome, the acrid taste of burning – of burnt buildings and burnt flesh – still lingered, heavy, in the air. Everywhere there hung the stench of death, as flies buzzed and circled over corpses, bloated, stinking, ugly in the dying August heat. And everywhere, Rome's people wandered helpless, disbelieving, traumatized and starving.

For there was no food in the city. The contents of the warehouses and granaries that lined the Tiber had been requisitioned by the Goths. For the Roman poor there was nothing left. But soon there would be nothing for the Goths either. Unless they moved with speed, they would be trapped and forced to spend the winter in a hostile unforgiving land.

Of course, the Goths knew where to go. If food would not be shipped to them from Africa, then they would take ship to Africa instead. And quickly, too. Autumn was fast approaching and, with every day that passed, the seas were becoming rougher and less auspicious for the voyage.

How they hoped to transport so many people, animals and possessions across the sea, cannot be guessed. But that was their intention.[105] With their wagons laden, heavy with the spoils of Rome, not only jewels and gold, but people too – the young princess, Galla Placidia, and the deposed emperor Attalus – the caravan snaked slowly out along the Appian Way to Capua, a wealthy agricultural city and useful staging post (*fig.* 10.6). Whether they sacked Capua is not known. It is likely that they tried – it was a city renowned for its luxury. Nearby Nola was ransacked.

And so from Capua – leaving a trail of destruction throughout the countryside of Campania and Lucania – the Gothic wagon train wound south, lumbering down the Popilian Way to Rhegium (Reggio di Calabria) and the sea on the southernmost tip of Italy. Here, the Goths stayed for some time, with Sicily clearly visible, tantalizingly close across the Straits of Messina. We can only guess what was happening during those days, as boats and ships were requisitioned and preparations made for crossing and over-wintering in Sicily.

Eventually, the embarkation began and the first ships put out to sea. But it was already too late. The sea was choppy, and the

Rome taken

wind and waves were rising rapidly. As Alaric and the rest of his Gothic army watched anxiously from the shoreline, the ships began to pitch and heave, to take in water, wallow and then, one by one, to sink. They would not try again.

Now, trapped in the farthest extremity of Italy and taunted by an angry sea, Alaric himself fell ill. Carried in a wagon, he led his people a little way back north until they reached the ancient city of Consentia. It was here a few days later that he died.

His people's grief was extravagant, his funeral elaborate. Jordanes' account of the event may be pure fiction. Or it may be true. But if true, the tomb and its treasures have never been found:

> His people mourned him with the greatest devotion. Near the city of Consentia, the life-giving waters of the River Busentus tumble down from the foot of the mountain. After diverting the river from its course, his people gathered a workforce of captives…to dig a grave for Alaric in the middle of the riverbed. At the centre of this pit, they buried their leader, surrounded by many treasures. Then they turned back the waters of the river to flow along its old course. So that no one should ever know exactly where Alaric was buried, they killed everyone who had dug his grave.[106]

# Epilogue

# CHAPTER 11

# *Shockwaves*

*As long as the Colosseum stands, so long stands Rome. But when it falls, then Rome falls and with it the whole world.*

(Attributed to the Venerable Bede, eighth century)

News of Rome's sack spread quickly. When it reached Ravenna, it was met with disbelief. Legend has it that at first the emperor Honorius simply could not take in the news. He heard from one of his eunuchs,

Bronze coin of the Ostrogothic king Theodahad (d. 536), struck at Rome in 534–6 (see also *fig. 11.6*).

who must have been the keeper of the poultry, that Rome was no more. Honorius groaned aloud and said, 'But it was eating from my hand a moment ago!' For he had a very large cockerel, which he called 'Rome'. When the eunuch realized Honorius' mistake, he told him that it was the city Rome that had perished at the hands of Alaric.

The story did the rounds, and was soon embellished by Honorius' detractors: 'The emperor sighed with relief and said, "My friend, I thought that my bird, Rome, had died!" Such, they say, was the emperor's stupidity.'[107]

How he reacted to the news of Alaric's death is not recorded. Acclaimed unanimously by the Goths, the kingship passed to Alaric's brother-in-law, the warlord known to the Romans as Ataulfus, but in his own tongue as Athavulf (Noble Wolf). In both appearance and intellect he was 'outstanding...for although physically he was not especially large, his body was very fine and his face most handsome'.[108] After abandoning all hope of a sea crossing in early 411, Ataulf led his people back along the roads that they had last travelled in the long hot days of summer after the sack of Rome.

'And, like a plague of locusts, [Ataulf] stripped all Italy bare of anything that still remained, not merely private wealth, but public, too; and there was nothing that Honorius could do to stop him.'[110]

And so, after a brief stop in Rome, he journeyed north past Florence and Milan and then across the Alps to Gaul, where one by one its cities fell to him: Marseilles, Bordeaux, Toulouse, and Narbonne. Gaul was a province sapped by conflict. Only months before had it been regained for Honorius by his general Constantius,[109] who had laid siege to the usurper Constantine III in Arles. Gradually deprived of reinforcements and supplies, Constantine finally took off the purple robes (which he had been sent by Honorius just a year before), and entered a church, where he was promptly ordained as a priest. But holy orders did not protect him. Constantine was arrested and sent with his son to Ravenna. But before they could reach the city, they were killed, and their heads sent for permanent exhibition on the walls of Carthage.

But already that year another usurper had arisen to take Constantine's place. Jovinus, a Gallo-Roman senator, had been proclaimed at Mainz, supported by the kings of the Burgundians and Alans, who had crossed the frozen Rhine four years before in 406.

At first, on the advice of Attalus, who had himself once briefly known what it was to be a usurping emperor, Ataulf threw his weight behind Jovinus. But things soon went sour. Ataulf discovered that another Goth was travelling to Jovinus' aid: Sarus, his sworn enemy, whose attack had sabotaged the peace talks at Ravenna just a year before. Now Sarus had quarrelled with Honorius and was riding through Gaul with a small band of followers. It was the chance Ataulf had prayed for. At the head of 10,000 Goths, he rode out in pursuit of Sarus. After a dramatic breakneck chase, Ataulf's horsemen captured Sarus with lassoes. He did not live much longer.

It was not long before Ataulf switched sides. Perhaps believing Sarus' enemy was his friend, he made overtures to Honorius, which the emperor accepted. For a few years, all seemed well between Ravenna and the Goths. Ataulf's change of heart, told in his own words, was reported to St Jerome in Bethlehem by a visitor from the western empire:

> He said that, at first, he had wanted passionately to obliterate
> the name of Rome and make the whole empire Gothic both
> in name and in fact... and that he, Ataulf, should become
> what Caesar Augustus had once been. But, through long
> experience, he had discovered that the Goths are unable to
> obey any law because of their unbridled barbarism. Believing
> that the state should not be deprived of laws (without which
> a state is not a state), he decided to gain glory for himself –
> by using the strength of his Goths to restore and increase
> the reputation of Rome – so that posterity might call him
> the architect of Rome's restoration, since there was nothing
> he could do to change it. So he did all he could to turn his
> back on fighting and to strive for peace.[111]

In 413, Ataulf proved his loyalty. At Valentia, he caught up with the army of Jovinus and defeated it. The imperial usurper, once captured, was sent to Narbonne, where he was executed. Jovinus' head, together with that of his lieutenant, was despatched to Africa to join those of Constantine III and his son on the walls of Carthage.

But Africa, too, had been in turmoil. Its commander, Heraclian, had revolted, fearful perhaps of reports that the Roman general Constantius was hunting down the enemies of Stilicho. As Stilicho's killer, Heraclian knew that he would be high on the hit list. Already, another of Stilicho's arch-rivals, the eunuch Olympius, had been arrested. Before being beaten to death – the fate he had so often meted out to others – his ears had been hacked off. Seizing the initiative, Heraclian once again cut off the corn supply to Italy and led his troops against Rome in 413. It was a short-lived but bloody rebellion. By the time it was over – and Heraclian had been killed – its consequences had become enormous.

For one thing, the supplies of food – which Ataulf had been promised, and for which he had agreed to hand back the princess Galla Placidia – had not come through. Placidia stayed put.[112] For another, as a reward for his services in saving Rome, the general Constantius had been given all Heraclian's estates in Africa, a vast wealth. Not only was Constantius now very rich, he was also very powerful, having been appointed consul, in recognition of Rome's gratitude.

But a jealousy had sprung up between Ataulf and Constantius. It cannot have been eased by Ataulf stealing the glory from Constantius in what he might have regarded as his own war against Jovinus. Constantius' jealousy was fanned to hatred when he heard of Ataulf's marriage. For in the first days of 414, a lavish ceremony was held in Narbonne to celebrate the wedding of the Gothic king to his beautiful young captive, the sister of Honorius – Galla Placidia.

> In a columned hall, Placidia sat decorated in full Roman imperial style, and beside her sat Ataulf dressed in the uniform and accoutrements of a Roman general. At the ceremony, among the other wedding gifts that Ataulf gave her were fifty handsome youths, all dressed in silk, each holding high two massive plates. One of these plates was piled with gold, the other with precious – in fact priceless – jewels: the jewels that the Goths had carried off from the sack of Rome.[113]

The marriage hymn was sung by none other than Priscus Attalus. It was all too much for Constantius. Having met Placidia before, he too now desired her as his wife. So he deliberately poisoned relations between the court and Ataulf, and soon gained permission to move against the Goth. He blockaded all seaports in the south of Gaul and prepared to attack.

Betrayed by Ravenna, Ataulf turned to history for a solution. He appointed an emperor of his own, one who already had experience of challenging Honorius. In 414, for the second time in five years, Priscus Attalus was elevated to the purple. But, as before, his reign would be short-lived. As Constantius regained control of Gaul, the Goths abandoned Attalus. He was captured and returned to Rome, where he was led through the streets in what would be the final triumph ever celebrated in the city. At its climax,

> Honorius ordered Attalus to stand on the first step of the tribunal... He cut off two fingers from his right hand, the [thumb][114] and forefinger. Then he banished him to the island of Lipara, doing nothing more to harm him, but rather ensuring that he had all the necessities of life.[115]

It was the very treatment that Jovius had suggested Honorius endure, when the emperor had almost abdicated in favour of Attalus back in 410. The mutilation was symbolic as was the exile, but Attalus would not live long on Lipara. He died the next year in 415.

By then, Ataulf, too, was dead. But before his time came, he had led his people south from Gaul, fleeing across the Pyrenees to Spain, a province already overrun by the Vandals and the Suevi. Riding beside him in his wagon, his wife, Galla Placidia, cradled their newborn son named after his grandfather, Theodosius. But when they came near Barcelona, little Theodosius died. He was buried outside the city in a silver coffin.

There is nothing to suggest that the child was murdered, but Ataulf did have enemies, and it would not be long before they struck. In early 415, he was assassinated in his stables, where he had gone to inspect his horses. On the face of it, it was an act of vengeance for the death of a rival Gothic warlord, whom Ataulf had killed years before. But more than this, it seems to have been part of a well-planned coup. For although on his death-bed he passed his kingdom over to his brother, Wallia, urging him to hand back Placidia and make peace with the Romans, events took a different course. Another of his enemies, who had been waiting in the wings, now grabbed his chance. Singeric, the brother of Ataulf's old enemy Sarus, took his revenge:

> Through treachery and force, rather than by lawful succession, Singeric became king. He killed Ataulf's children by his first marriage, tearing them by force from

the arms of Bishop Sigesarus. And out of malice against Ataulf, he ordered that his queen, Placidia, be made to walk in front of his horse, with the rest of the prisoners, in a procession of some twelve miles from the city.[116]

Eventually Wallia did return Placidia to the Romans, ransoming her for 600,000 measures of wheat, enough to feed 200,000 people for a month. For, although they had the wealth of Rome at their disposal, without access to food the Goths were nothing. In the end, a homeland of their own with enough to eat was all that they had ever really wanted. Compared with this, the silks and statuary of Rome were but a sideshow. The Goths remained in Gaul for almost a hundred years before the Franks invaded, forcing them to move on again, this time to Spain (*fig.* 11.1).

After the machismo of the Gothic camp, the wagon trains, the battles and bravado, Ravenna must have seemed an oddly tame place to Placidia. With just the salt breeze stirring the silks strung between the pillars of the palace, the hushed courtyards were ruffled only by the clucking of her brother's hens.

She was not allowed her thoughts for long. Constantius had been badgering Honorius to let him marry her, and in 417 he agreed. What Placidia made of her new husband is anybody's guess. The picture sketched by the contemporary chronicler Olympiodorus is hardly prepossessing:

In public processions, Constantius was sullen and morose. He had bulging eyes, a thick neck and massive head. When riding he always slumped over his horse's neck, looking shiftily from side to side, so that he seemed to everyone to have (as the saying goes) 'a very tyrant's look'. But at dinner and at parties, he was witty and affable, and even competed with the mime-artists who often used to play before his table.[117]

But Placidia had two children by him and in 421, when Constantius became co-emperor with Honorius, she was granted the position of *Augusta*. Constantius lived for only another few months, Honorius for not much longer and, when he died in August 423, he left no heirs. His experience with Stilicho's two daughters had apparently left him so averse to wedlock that it was not an experience he ever wanted to repeat.

Placidia was now not only the widow of both a Visigothic king and Roman emperor, but the mother of a Roman emperor as well. When her infant son, Valentinian III, was helped onto the jewel-encrusted throne of the western empire, in 425, Placidia became his regent, one of the most powerful women in the world. For many years, as her son was growing up, she stayed on in Ravenna, supervising court life, intervening in disputes, building churches and attempting to control not only powerful generals but her own children too. But in 450, a crisis arose, and Placidia, now fifty-eight, travelled down to Rome.

As she passed through the city gates, along the streets, where emperors had once ridden in triumph, her mind must have returned to the confusion and carnage of those late August days forty years earlier. She may have reflected on how quickly the city seemed to have recovered. Much of its gold, its silver and its jewels, its boxes of spices and its bales of silks, may have been loaded onto Gothic wagons and taken far from Rome; part of its treasure, indeed, had formed her bridal gift from Ataulf in that dazzling display in Gaul thirty-six years earlier. But the fabric of the city still looked much the same.

The Forum had soon been restored. The great Basilica Julia, the Senate offices and the Baths of Sura on the Aventine, had quickly been rebuilt (*fig.* 11.2). The Colosseum still rose tall, as imposing and imperial as when Placidia had been a child. Restored twice since the sack, because of earthquakes, it remained as popular a venue now as ever, with its wild beast hunts drawing massive crowds. Nor had the Roman passion for

chariot racing lessened. On holidays, the Circus Maximus was still packed out. As she listened to the sound of the spectators, Placidia perhaps remembered the ear-splitting roar on that day in 404, when she had joined Honorius, Stilicho and her young fiancé, Eucherius, in the imperial box to watch the soldiers thrill the crowd with their manoeuvres.

But some things had changed. The streets were noticeably emptier. After the sack, and once security had been restored, Rome's numbers had appeared to stabilize. But then, in 439, the Vandals had taken Carthage, and the food supply had dried up. Now the number of people living, not only in Rome, but also in all Italy, was falling steadily (*fig* 11.3). In the countryside, an increasing number of farms and villas lay empty. In the city, whole districts were deserted. Over the last forty years, Rome's population had shrunk by almost half. In economic terms, the city was becoming sidelined. It was turning into something of a backwater.

Looking closer at the face of Rome, more changes could be seen. Some pagan temples were still standing – on the Capitoline, the gilded roof-tiles of the Temple of Jupiter still

**11.2** Two statue bases re-erected in the Basilica Julia in 416 (or 377) during the restoration of the building by the city prefect, Gabinius Vettius Probianus. The bases were intended for two classical statues, made by Polyclitus and Timarchus.

**11.3** This wall mosaic from Carthage, from the late 5th to early 6th century, probably represents a Vandal horseman before his villa in North Africa. The Vandals ruled over a prosperous kingdom until 533 when Belisarius reconquered the region for Justinian I. It was the Vandals who sacked Rome in 455, causing even more damage than Alaric's Goths.

glinted in the sunlight. But the marbles and pillars of other temples had been stripped to adorn the Christian churches that had sprung up across Rome: St John's Lateran, St Peter in Chains, and St Sabina (*fig. 3.5*).

Yet many palaces were comfortable still. Enough of the city's treasures had been spared or hidden from the Goths. It was just that the spirit of the place had changed. If Placidia had time, amidst the worries plaguing her, she might have reflected on the intellectual shifts that the sack had caused.

Even as the shockwaves from the sack of Rome were still reverberating through the empire, philosophers and theologians had begun to grapple with its existential consequences. For 800 years, Rome had been secure, inviolable, eternal. Now she had fallen.

For the pagans, the reasons for her fall were clear: she had rejected her old gods. The city might still be the 'mother of men and the mother of gods',[118] but Rome had abandoned her gods, who had, in turn, abandoned her. 'If Rome has not been saved by its gods,' they argued, 'it is because they are no longer there; as long as they were there, they kept the city safe'.[119]

But it was not only the pagans who were shocked. In Bethlehem, the notoriously cantankerous St Jerome, labouring over his translation of the Bible into Latin, was overwhelmed by the news. 'When the brightest light in all the world was quenched,' he wrote, 'when the head was taken from the Roman empire, when to say it all more accurately, the whole world fell in that one city's fall, I was struck dumb with silence. I kept silent even about what was good, and I was moved to sorrow.'[120]

After all, for the Christians, the sack had been potentially an even greater disaster than for the pagans. Rome was the heart of the western Christian faith, the city of St Peter and St Paul, the Papal See. If the pagan gods had failed to save a city that no longer worshipped them, where had the new God been when His city was sacked? And sacked by Christians at that! It was a powerful and disturbing argument, and one that exposed the new God's seeming impotence.

It was left to St Augustine to rise to the challenge (fig. 11.4). Although he was the son of a devout Christian mother, Augustine's own journey to conversion, mapped out in his *Confessions* (397), had been lengthy and contorted. Educated as a pagan, he taught rhetoric first in Carthage, then in Rome and Milan, becoming a strong adherent initially of Manicheism (a cult, obsessed with the battle between good and evil), then of the fashionable philosophy of neo-Platonism (traditional pagan thinking with a personal twist), before finally being converted to Christianity by Ambrose, bishop of Milan, in 386. Within five years, he was ordained as a priest, serving in the diocese of Hippo on the coast of Africa, just west of Carthage. Four years later, in 395 (the year in which Placidia's father, Theodosius, had died), Augustine was elevated to the bishopric, a position that he held until his death in 430.

In his great work, *The City of God* (413–26), Augustine defended the role of God in the destruction of Rome. God allowed Rome to be sacked, he argued, because it was an earthly city, a place that did not fully expound Justice and Virtue as

**11.4** *St Augustine Seated with a Book of Sermons,* print by Jacob Matham, after Giuseppe Cesari d'Arpino, Holland, 1600.

S. AVGVSTINVS.

*Iosephus Arpinas. pinxit.*
*Mathum sculp. et excud.*

*Plurima doctori Ambrosio, tibi debeo mater*
*Plurima, cuncta Deo, quorum sum munere tantus.*

only the spiritual celestial City of God could do.[121] Although Augustine did not reject attempts to build a just and virtuous city on earth, he argued that mankind should be more interested in preparing for the celestial city – the perfect Christian city to come.

Such sentiments may have consoled Placidia. But she had worries of a far more temporal kind. That spring a letter, whose contents were explosive, had been found from her own daughter, the headstrong Honoria. Unknown to the emperor or court and certainly unknown to her mother – but influenced perhaps by childhood stories of Placidia's adventures with the Goths – Honoria had written begging help from a barbarian king. Please would he come and rescue her? She was being forced into a marriage with a senator she did not love. If only the king would save her, she would gladly marry him – and as proof she enclosed with the letter a ring. The court was furious. The emperor demanded that she should die. Placidia defended her, but it was difficult, not least because the man, with whom Honoria had been corresponding, was the king of the invading Huns: Attila.

In the midst of growing turmoil, Galla Placidia died in Rome on 27 November 450. She was buried not in Ravenna, in the mausoleum she herself had built, but in the empire's ancient capital of Rome (fig. 11.5).

She would not see Attila's savage raids on Gaul and Italy in the next two years – raids that he would try to justify in part by quoting Honoria's letter. Neither would she see her son, the emperor Valentinian III, assassinated in a struggle with his generals; nor her granddaughter, Eudocia, traded in a power game with a Vandal king.

**11.5** The Mausoleum of Galla Placidia in Ravenna was built in c.425–50. But, after her death in Rome, her remains were apparently transferred to the Theodosian family vault in St Peter's, Rome. Exactly who is buried here remains a mystery. Although the building is complete, it has sunk about 1.5m into the ground.

**11.6** Bronze coin of the Ostrogothic king Theodahad, struck at Rome in 534–6. On the reverse, a classical Victory stands on a prow, between the letters 'S C' for *Senatus Consulto* (by the decree of the Senate). But the obverse shows Theodahad as a Gothic king with his distinctive helmet and moustache.

And then, not five years after Placidia had died, Rome was sacked again. For fourteen days, the Vandals stripped the city of whatever still remained, ripping the gilded roof-tiles from the Temple of Jupiter on the Capitoline, loading gold and statues, all that was left of the imperial treasures, onto ships bound south for Carthage.[122]

The western empire was collapsing. Britain had long gone. Now Spain, Gaul and Africa lay in barbarian hands. Only Italy remained, and soon even she would be lost. Further waves of barbarian warlords once again scrambled for Rome until in 476 the last Roman emperor of the west,[123] the feeble Romulus Augustulus, was forced from power by the Hunnic chieftain Odovacer. The imperial insignia were rapidly bundled up and sent east under guard to Constantinople. Four years later, governed by a barbarian king, Italy officially became a province of the eastern empire.

# Aftermath:
# Rome AD 410–575

After the last Roman emperor was deposed from office in 476, any
claim that Rome might once have had to be the capital of the Roman
Empire was lost. Ravenna was now supreme. It was from here that Italy
would be governed: first in 476, by Odovacer the Hun; then, in 493,
by Theodoric, the Ostrogoth.

Theodoric was acknowledged by the Senate and scrupulous in his
service of the eastern emperor, Anastasius. He governed Italy for thirty-
three years, during which time he further embellished his capital,
Ravenna. Among other projects he built a new baptistery, a church –
St Apollinaire Nuovo – and his own mausoleum.

But Rome remained important. Theodoric visited the city in 500
and saw to the restoration of the Theatre of Marcellus in 507–11. He
probably presided over the games, which were still recorded as taking
place in the Colosseum as late as 523. Moreover, as Theodoric respected
the Senate in Rome, some of its members, such as Boethius and
Cassiodorus, gained high positions in his government (*fig.* 11.6).

But the population of Rome had shrunk significantly, from around
perhaps 800,000 just before 410 to about 15,000 in 530. The fall in
numbers was for the most part due to the decline of free food, the
supply from Carthage having been cut off permanently in 439. Even
so, some wheat, meat and wine continued to be imported by the
government of Rome from Sicily and other parts of Italy, and so
the city carried on.

But the relative peace of early sixth-century Italy was shattered in
535 by the invasion of a Byzantine army from the eastern empire, under
the command of Count Belisarius. Having just retaken Africa from the
Vandals, Belisarius was tasked by his emperor Justinian I (*fig.* 8.2) with
recapturing Italy from the Ostrogoths. Over the next two decades,
Rome would change hands no fewer than four times before Narses,
Justinian's eunuch general, finally took the city in 552. Of several sieges
that took place during the Gothic War, the most devastating occurred

in 547, when the Ostrogothic king Totila, destroyed many buildings, including parts of the circuit walls. According to one chronicler, the city was left depopulated for forty days.

In 568, another barbarian people, the Lombards, took control of Italy. By now, Rome's chief importance lay in its role as the papal seat, but it was a role that would ultimately ensure its survival. By the time of Pope Gregory the Great (590–604), the Eternal City had been transformed. From having been the political seat of the greatest empire the ancient world had ever seen, it had become the spiritual centre of Christianity. Its new role was consolidated by Pope Gregory in 595, when he sent his own Augustine west from Rome to convert the barbarians on the coldest frontiers of the now disintegrated empire – on a mission that began in the lost Roman province of Britannia.

In his missionary zeal, Gregory had perhaps read the words of the pagan Greek Eunapius describing the sack of Rome two centuries earlier:

> It was obvious to everyone that, if the Roman Empire had shunned luxury and embraced war, there was nothing in all the world it could not have conquered and enslaved. But God has infected man's nature with a lethal characteristic, like the poisonous gall in a lobster or thorns upon a rose…[124]

# Who's Who in AD 410

*All dates are AD.*

**Alaric** (King of the Visigoths, r. 395–410/11) served as general of the Goths under Theodosius I at the Battle of the River Frigidus in 394. He became king of the Goths a year later when his people were residing in the Balkans. He subsequently became involved in the political machinations between the western and eastern imperial courts. Alaric led the Goths into Italy in 401–2, but was driven out a year later by Stilicho. A failure to gain lands and recognition from Honorius provoked another invasion of Italy in 408, resulting in the sack of Rome in 410. Alaric then led the Goths south in order to invade Africa; this venture failed and Alaric died in southern Italy soon afterwards.

**Anastasius** (r. 491–518) was a successful ruler of the eastern empire. Ruling from Constantinople, he maintained some influence in Italy through Odovacer and then Theodoric the Ostrogoth, who were both prepared to rule in the name of the Roman emperor. In reality, however, Italy lay outside the effective reach of Constantinople's power.

**Arbogast** (d. 394) was a Frankish general in the western Roman army. Although regarded as a loyal and honest leader, he was a pagan. He ultimately rebelled against Theodosius I and placed his puppet, Eugenius, on the throne. Both died after the Battle of the River Frigidus, Arbogast falling on his own sword.

**Arcadius** (r. 383–408) was the eldest son of Theodosius I, and brother of Honorius. A junior emperor under his father, he then reigned as emperor of the eastern empire from 395 to 408.

**Ataulf** (King of the Visigoths, 411–15) succeeded his brother-in-law, Alaric, in 411 and led the Goths out of Italy into Gaul, where they settled in Aquitaine. He married Theodosius I's daughter Galla Placidia, in 414, and made Priscus Attalus emperor for a second time in the same year. Ataulf failed to gain the concessions from Rome, namely land and food, which his people needed. His failure caused dissatisfaction among his followers and contributed to his assassination by fellow Goths.

**Attila the Hun** (d. 453) has come down in history as the 'scourge' of the Romans. Ruling the Huns from *c*.440 to 453, he caused devastation in both the eastern and western halves of the empire. One of his reasons for invading the west was the letter he had received from Honoria, the daughter of Gallia Placidia, asking him to rescue her from an unwanted marriage; however, unlike her mother, she did not marry a barbarian king. His death in 453 led to the break up of the Hunnic Empire.

**Constantine I** (r. 306–37) was made emperor unconstitutionally at York in Britain, after the death of his father, Constantius I. After defeating Maxentius at the Battle of the Milvian Bridge in 312, he became joint emperor with Licinius. Together they issued the 'Edict of Toleration' at Milan in 313, which led to an end of the persecutions of Christians. In 324, Constantine defeated Licinius and became sole emperor. He dedicated his new city, Constantinople, in 330.

**Constantine III** (r. 407–11) was declared emperor unconstitutionally in Britain, after the short reigns of the usurpers Marcus and Gratian. He took the British army to the Continent and defeated both the barbarians and Honorius' army under Sarus. He gained control of Spain, Gaul and Germany and based his court at Arles.

**Constantius I** (r. 293–306) (also known as Constantius Chlorus) was a junior emperor in the original Tetrarchy of Diocletian. He became senior emperor in 305, but died a year later in York. He was succeeded by his son Constantine I.

**Constantius II** (r. 324–61) was a son of Constantine I. He became a senior emperor in 337 and ruled in the east. A particularly strict and remote ruler, he largely set the trend for the nature of imperial rule in the following century.

**Constantius III** (r. 421) rose from a soldier of humble birth to become the pre-eminent general of the western empire in the latter part of Honorius' reign. He was responsible for the demise of Constantine III and also had successes against barbarians. In 417, he married Galla Placidia; their son became Valentinian III. Constantius was himself emperor for seven months before his premature death.

**Diocletian** (r. 284–305) came to the throne when the Roman Empire had suffered heavily as a result of barbarian invasions, civil war and inflation. His reforms strengthened the frontiers, created a new form of civil service and even changed the coinage. He set the empire on a new footing that ensured its survival. In 305 he retired to his fortified palace at Split, where his favourite activity was growing cabbages.

**Eucherius** (d. 408), the son of Stilicho and Serena, was betrothed to Galla Placidia. It was the rumour that Stilicho intended Eucherius to become emperor of the east after the death of Arcadius that signalled the fall of Stilicho. After Stilicho's death, Eucherius was murdered.

**Eudoxia** (d. 404) was the daughter of a Frank of consular rank. She married Arcadius in 395, becoming empress in 400. Among her children were the future emperor Theodosius II and the influential Pulcheria, future consort to the emperor Marcian. Eudoxia was heavily involved in the politics of both Church and state until her early death.

**Eugenius** (r. 392–4) was a pagan rhetorician who worked in the western imperial bureaucracy. He was made emperor by the barbarian general Arbogast in a challenge to Theodosius I. He was executed after his defeat at the Battle of the River Frigidus in 394.

**Eutropius** (d. *c*.400), a eunuch, was an Assyrian slave who rose to become a leading minister in the court of Arcadius from 395 to 399. He was instrumental in the fall of his predecessor, Rufinus, and a rival of his western counterpart, Stilicho. The first eunuch to be made consul in 399, he was overthrown in the same year and banished to Cyprus.

**Fritigern** (d. *c*.380) was one of the Gothic kings who led his people across the Danube in 376. He became the leader of the Gothic army in the Balkans and was responsible for the defeat of Valens at the Battle of Hadrianople in 378.

**Gainas** (d. 400–1), a Gothic general in the eastern empire, was instrumental in the downfall of Rufinus in 395. Later, he colluded with the Goths in Asia Minor and his men briefly occupied Constantinople in 400. He was hounded out by another Gothic general, Fravitta, and was finally defeated and killed by the Huns under Uldin in 400–1.

**Galerius** (r. 293–311) was originally a junior emperor in Diocletian's Tetrarchy. In 303, with the decrees against Christians, Galerius became one of the most fervent persecutors. He relented shortly before his very painful death, an event celebrated by the Christian writer, Lactantius.

**Galla Placidia** (c.388–450) was the daughter of Theodosius I and half-sister of Honorius and Arcadius. Under the guardianship of Stilicho and Serena, she was betrothed to their son Eucherius. She supported the execution of Serena in 408. After the sack of Rome, she was taken hostage by Alaric and stayed with the Goths until she married Ataulf in Gaul in 414. After his death in 415, she returned to Ravenna and married Constantius III. Their son became the emperor Valentinian III and their daughter Honoria corresponded controversially with Attila the Hun in 450. Placidia was the power behind her son's throne until her death in 450.

**Generid** (fl. early 5th century) was a barbarian general in the western empire who served under Honorius. He was promoted in 409, when Honorius repealed the law that pagans could not be generals.

**Gildo** (d. 398) was a Moor who was made commander of North Africa in 397 by the eunuch Eutropius, who ran the eastern empire on behalf of Arcadius. In response, Stilicho quickly recruited Gildo's estranged brother Mascezel, who invaded Carthage and defeated Gildo in 398.

**Gratian** (r. 367–83) was the son of Valentinian I (364–75), who made him emperor in the west. Gratian had several successes against the barbarians, but strained relations with his uncle Valens meant that his army was not present at the Battle of Hadrianople in 378. He was finally overthrown and killed by Magnus Maximus.

**Helena (St Helena of Constantinople)** (c.255–c.330) was the mother of Constantine I, the first Christian emperor of Rome. She converted to Christianity after her son, but became a zealous supporter of the new faith. Helena visited the Holy Land in 326 and founded churches on the Mount of Olives in Jerusalem, and at Bethlehem. She was also reputed to have found the True Cross on which Christ was crucified. She was the first high-profile woman to patronize Christianity; many were to follow.

**Heraclian** (d. 413) was responsible for the murder of Stilicho in 408. Honorius rewarded him by making him commander of North Africa. Based at Carthage, he was responsible for the grain supply to Rome, withholding it from the usurping emperor Atallus in 409/10. Heraclian made an attempt to become emperor in 413, but was defeated between Ostia and Rome; he fled back to Carthage where he was executed.

**Honorius** (r. 393–423) was the second son of Theodosius I. He inherited the western empire, but was under the control of Stilicho until 408. He fled Milan for Ravenna in 402, effectively making it the capital of the west. He successively married both daughters of Stilicho, Maria and Thermantia, but had no children by either. Despite several usurpations and numerous barbarian invasions during his reign, he managed to survive until he died of natural causes; he achieved very little apart from breeding chickens.

**Innocent I** (r. 402–17) played an important role in negotiations between Alaric and Honorius, visiting Ravenna on a diplomatic mission. However, he was also to ensure that Rome gained much more influence in ecclesiastical matters, successfully challenging eastern Church leaders. His papacy demonstrated how the pope in Rome was increasingly becoming the dominant character in the city in late Roman times.

**Jovinus** (r. 411–13), a Gaulish noble of senatorial rank, was a usurper raised to the purple by the Burgundian king Guntiarius and the Alan king Goar. Although he received initial support from the Visigothic king Ataulf, their relationship later broke down. Changing his allegiance to Honorius, Ataulf captured Jovinus and handed him over to Dardanus, prefect of the Gauls, at Narbonne. Jovinus was executed after only two years' rule.

**Jovius** (*fl.* early 5th century) was an established member of Roman society. In 405 he was made praetorian prefect of Illyricum by Stilicho, and befriended Alaric. He became praetorian prefect of Italy in 409 and was behind the revolt at Ravenna in the same year. He negotiated with

Alaric, but was let down by Honorius, who would not accept the terms agreed. He briefly left Honorius to serve under Priscus Attalus, but later persuaded Alaric to strip Attalus of the purple in 410.

**Julian the Apostate** (r. 355–63) was not only the last of Constantine I's family to be emperor, he was also the last pagan ruler who tried to turn back the tide of Christianity. He was unsuccessful.

**Justinian I** (r. 527–65) Justinian the Great was the most successful of the early eastern Roman, or Byzantine, emperors. Famous for the rebuilding of the church of Hagia Sophia in Constantinople, he also tried to reconquer the west. In 533, his general, Count Belisarius, regained Africa from the Vandals; from 533 to 552, Belisarius and then the eunuch Narses conducted a long war with the Ostrogoths in Italy. Although the Byzantine emperor regained Italy, the peninsula suffered enormous damage; furthermore, within just a few years, in 568, the Lombards would wrench Italy from Byzantium. However, this was not before a wonderful wall mosaic showing Justinian and his court was added to the church of San Vitale in Ravenna (*fig.* 8.2).

**Magnus Maximus** (r. 383–8) was a governor of Britain who usurped against Theodosius I. He ruled over Spain, Gaul, Britain and Germany for five years before being defeated by Theodosius in 388.

**Marcella** (325–410) was a member of a noble Roman family. She lost her husband when she was young, after which she devoted her life to Christ. She made her palace on the Aventine Hill an early form of convent, where women led an ascetic life and carried out charitable activities. Jerome called her 'the glory of the ladies of Rome'. She was brutalized by the barbarians in 410, dying soon afterwards in the sanctuary of St Peter's.

**Maria** (d. 407) was the elder daughter of Stilicho and Serena. Married to Honorius in 398, she had no children.

**Mascezel** (*fl.* late 4th century) overthrew his estranged brother, Gildo, commander of Africa, in 398, at the behest of Stilicho.

**Melania the Younger** (*c.*383–438) came from a wealthy senatorial family in Rome and she inherited estates in Britain, Spain, Africa and Italy. Just before the sack, she fled Rome with her young husband for Africa, where she became a friend of St Augustine. Later, she travelled east and founded religious establishments in Jerusalem and encouraged the empress Eudocia, the wife of Theodosius II, to patronize works in the Holy Land.

**Odovacer** (r. 476-93) Odovacer's father was a close associate of Attila the Hun. After the break-up of the Hunnic Empire, Odovacer arrived in Italy. Gaining the support of the army, he deposed the last ruling emperor of the west, Romulus Augustulus, in 476. Odovacer ruled Italy from his capital in Ravenna, although he acknowledged the eastern emperor at Constantinople. Odovacer was deposed and killed by the next ruler of Italy, Theodoric the Ostrogoth.

**Olympius** (d. *c.*?411–15) was promoted to high office by Stilicho. He subsequently turned against his benefactor and was the architect of his fall in 408. He then became Honorius' leading minister and obsessively persecuted all those connected with Stilicho. In 409 he led a daring raid on Ataulf's army, but in the end was expelled from Ravenna later in 409, as a result of intrigue among the court eunuchs. He was finally executed by Constantius III.

**Palladius** (d. after 421), a junior senator, was made responsible for raising payments in Rome to pay off Alaric's demands in 408. He held a senior post in Africa in 410 and became consul in 416.

**Priscus Attalus** (r. 409–10 and 414–5) was an experienced senator. He led a diplomatic mission to Honorius in Ravenna, as a result of which he was made prefect of Rome during Alaric's siege of 409. Alaric made him emperor, as a rival to Honorius, hoping that this would finally break the deadlock in his negotiations with the Roman authorities. Attalus, however, did not fully cooperate with Alaric and was deposed in 410; however, he subsequently stayed with the Goths until Ataulf made him emperor again in 414. He sang the marriage hymn at the wedding of Ataulf and Galla Placidia. After falling from power in 415, Attalus was sent to Rome, mutilated by order of the court and banished to the Island of Lipara, where he died shortly afterwards.

**Radagaisus** (d. 406) was an Ostrogothic king, who led an invasion across the Rhine and Danube in 405. His force reached Florence, but was repelled and defeated by Stilicho, the final action occurring at

Fiesole in 406. Prisoners taken were incorporated into the Roman army; many were to side with Alaric a few years later.

**Rufinus** (d. 395) was the praetorian prefect in the east when Theodosius I died in 395. He effectively took control of the government on behalf of the young emperor Arcadius, holding off Stilicho's attempts to gain control of Constantinople. A plot involving Gainas in 395 led to Rufinus' assassination outside the walls of Constantinople.

**Sarus** (d. *c.*412) may have been Alaric's unsuccessful rival for the Gothic kingship in 395. He served as a general in the western empire. In 407 he was sent by Stilicho on an unsuccessful campaign against the usurper Constantine III. His sudden raid on Alaric outside Ravenna derailed the last attempt at negotiations and led to the sack of Rome in 410. He was finally killed in Gaul by Ataulf *c.*412, but his brother, Singeric, gained revenge by assassinating Ataulf in 415.

**Serena** (d. 408) was the niece and ward of Theodosius I, who gave her in marriage to Stilicho. She was instrumental in betrothing her son, Eucherius, to Galla Placidia. After Stilicho's disgrace and death in 408, she was condemned to death by the Senate.

**Stilicho** (d. 408) was the son of a Vandal father and Roman mother. He rose to prominence as a general under Theodosius I and played an important role in the defeat of the usurper Eugenius at the Battle of the River Frigidus in 394. He subsequently married Theodosius' niece Serena. From 395 to 408, Stilicho effectively ruled the western empire for Honorius, an alliance that he strengthened through marriage ties – Honorius was married to Stilicho's daughters, Maria and Thermantia, while Honorius' half-sister Galla Placidia was betrothed to Stilicho's son, Eucherius. Stilicho had numerous dealings with Alaric and his Goths. He was finally killed by Heraclian in a *coup-d'etat*, masterminded by Olympius.

**Symmachus** (*c.*340–*c.*402) was a pagan senator steeped in Classical learning. He served in Africa and was prefect of Rome in 384–5. The last great pagan senator of Rome, he led the opposition to the removal of the Altar of Victory from the Senate House, in 382, but was ultimately defeated by Ambrose, bishop of Milan. He wrote a large number of letters to many of the famous characters of the day, including Stilicho.

**Theodoric the Ostrogoth** (r. 493-526) was one of the most successful barbarian kings. He governed Italy, ostensibly for the eastern empire, for three decades. It was a period of relative peace after the turmoil of much of the fifth century. Although Theodoric ruled from Ravenna, where he built a church and baptistery, he did visit Rome and respected the city's position in Italy. Two of his senior government officials, Boethius and Cassiodorus, were drawn from the ranks of the Senate.

**Theodosius I** (r. 379–95) himself the son of a famous general, was re-called from an early retirement by Gratian to fight the Goths in the Balkans after the Battle of Hadrianople in 378. He became the emperor of the eastern part of the empire, and in 382 made a treaty with the Goths. In 391, he banned all pagan practices, making Christianity the state religion of the empire. On his death, he divided the empire between his sons, Honorius and Arcadius.

**Theodosius II** (r. 402–50), the son of Arcadius, became emperor when only nine months old. For much of his reign, he was heavily influenced by his elder sister, Pulcheria, who was an empress in her own right from 414 to 453. Theodosius' reign saw the eastern empire survive the onslaught of the Huns, partly achieved by the famous land-walls of Constantinople – the Theodosian Walls, named after him to this day.

**Thermantia** (d. 415) was the younger daughter of Stilicho and Serena. She was married to Honorius in 408 after the death of his first wife, Thermantia's sister Maria. Soon after, Stilicho was murdered. Honorius divorced Thermantia and returned her to her mother Serena.

**Valens** (r. 364–78) ruled as co-emperor with his brother Valentinian I. Valens was an Arian and also a highly irascible character. It was his incompetence in dealing with the Gothic threat that led to the disastrous defeat of the Roman eastern field army at the Battle of Hadrianople, in 378, where he was killed.

**Valens** (d. 410) was a general of Honorius who attacked Alaric in January 409, losing 6,000 men. He managed to escape to Rome, where he became a general for Priscus Attalus, but was executed for treason by Alaric.

**Valentinian I** (r. 364–75) ruled as co-emperor alongside his brother Valens. Valentinian had to fight several campaigns against barbarians in the west and actually died of a seizure brought on by anger whilst negotiating with a disingenuous barbarian deputation. His son, Gratian, was to continue his successful campaigning in the west.

**Valentinian II** (r. 375–92), another son of Valentinian I, was only four when made emperor. For most of his reign he was either marginalized or under the protection of Theodosius I. His apparent suicide led to Arbogast, the Frankish general, making Eugenius emperor in the west in 392.

**Valentinian III** (r. 425–55) was the son of Galla Placidia and Constantius III. He was made emperor of the west by the eastern court and ruled largely under the influence of his mother. He was assassinated only five years after her death in 450.

# Original sources

**Ammianus Marcellinus** (*c.*330–95) was a Greek from Antioch who served on the eastern frontier and in Gaul. He retired to Rome in 378, where he wrote his *Histories* covering the period 96–378. Only the part for 353–78 survives, but this provides essential background for the decline of Rome. Although he was a pagan, he was not openly hostile to Christianity.

> *Ammianus Marcellinus: The Later Roman Empire (AD 354–378)* (trans. W. Hamilton) (Penguin Classics 1986).
> J.C. Rolfe, *Ammianus Marcellinus: History* (Loeb 1989).

**Augustine (St)** (354–430) was born at Thagaste (in modern Algeria) to a Christian mother. He taught rhetoric at Carthage, Rome and Milan, and took up Manicheism before finally converting to Christianity in 386 under Ambrose, bishop of Milan. He was ordained a priest at Hippo (in modern Algeria) in 391 before becoming bishop in 395. His response to the fall of Rome is encapsulated in his most famous work, *City of God* (413–26).

> St Augustine, *Confessions* (trans. R. S. Pine-Coffin) (Penguin Classics 1961).
> St Augustine, *City of God* (trans. H. Bettenson) (Penguin Classics 1984).

**Ausonius** (d. *c.*395) taught rhetoric and grammar in Bordeaux before he was summoned to be the tutor of Gratian (emperor 367–83). He was to become governor of Gaul and was then made a consul. His various letters and works of prose and poetry provide insights into the period before the sack of Rome.

> H.G.E. White, *Ausonius* (Loeb 1919).

**Claudian (Claudius Claudianus)** (d. *c.*404) was from Alexandria. He had arrived in Rome by 395 and became a court poet for Honorius and a favourite of Stilicho. He was so famous that he was honoured with a statue before his death. His poems, including those about Stilicho and Honorius, contain important information about the Roman court and its activities just prior to the fall of Rome.

Maurice Platnauer, *Claudian* (Loeb 1963).

**Eunapius** (*c.*345–after 414) was a sophist and vehement pagan from Sardis (in modern Turkey). He continued the *History* of Dexippus that ended in 270, taking it up to 404. Only fragments of his work survive, but he was a major source for Zosimus and the Christian writers Sozomen, Socrates and Philostorgius.

R. Blockley, *The Fragmentary Classicising Historians of the Later Roman Empire – Eunapius, Olympiodorus, Priscus and Malchus* II (Text, Translation and Historiographical Notes), ARCA Classical and Medieval Texts, Papers and Monographs 10 (Francis Cairns 1983).

**Eusebius of Caesarea** (*c.*260–*c.*340) is regarded as the 'Father of Church History'. He witnessed the persecutions in Palestine between 303 and 310 during the reign of Diocletian. He ultimately became Bishop of Caesarea, and an advisor to Constantine on the Arian controversy. He wrote a large number of works of which the two most important for this book are his *Ecclesiastical History* (*c.*325) and *Life of Constantine* (*c.*337–40).

K. Lake and J.E.L. Oulton, *Ecclesiastical History* (Loeb 1926–32).

Eusebius, *The History of the Church* (trans. G.A. Williamson) (Penguin Classics 1965).

A. Cameron and S. Hall, *Eusebius' The Life of Constantine* (Clarendon Press 1999).

**Isidore of Seville** (*c.*602–36) was bishop of Seville and a prolific writer who drew upon many ancient sources. Among his works were a *Chronicle* (*c.*615) and a *History of the Goths* (*c.*624).

Stephen A. Barney, W.J. Lewis, J.A. Beach and Oliver Berghof (trans.), *The Etymologies of Isidore of Seville* (Cambridge University Press 2006).

**Jerome (St)** (*c.*342–420) was born near Aquileia, in northern Italy. He became a Christian in Rome before moving to the Levant, where he lived an ascetic life and learnt Hebrew. In 386 he moved to Bethlehem, where he founded a monastery and translated the Bible into Latin (*Vulgate*). His letters contain important responses to the sack of Rome.

http://www.ccel.org/ccel/schaff/npnf206.toc.html

**John the Lydian** (or John Lydus) (*c*.490–*c*.554 or later), a senior civil servant in the eastern empire, worked in Constantinople. His work *On the Magistracies of the Roman State* opens up many of the secrets of late Roman bureaucracy. The most accessible accounts of John's work appear in Kelly 2004 (q.v.).

**Jordanes** (*fl. c*.550) was probably of Gothic origin from somewhere on the River Danube. He served as a notary to a Gothic chief. He wrote a history of the Goths, *The Origin and Deeds of the Getae*, which was largely based on a work by Cassiodorus (*c*.490–583), who served the Ostrogothic kings of Italy.
  C.C. Mierow, *The Gothic History of Jordanes* (Princeton 1915, reprinted 2006).

**Juvenal** (*fl. c*.50/65–127 or later) wrote sixteen surviving satires, which give a vivid insight into the daily life of ancient Rome.
  P. Green, *Juvenal, The Sixteen Satires* (Penguin 2004).

**Lactantius** (*c*.240–320) was a teacher of rhetoric under Diocletian at Nicomedia. He converted to Christianity in around 300 and became tutor to Constantine's son, Crispus. Lactantius wrote several important Christian treatises, his *Divine Institutes* (304–11) and *On the Deaths of the Persecutors* (*c*.318) being the most famous.
  R.M. Ogilvie, *The Library of Lactantius* (Clarendon Press 1978).
  *On the Deaths of the Persecutors:*
    http://www.ccel.org/ccel/schaff/anf07.toc.html
  *The Divine Institutes*: http://www.ccel.org/ccel/schaff/anf07.toc.html

**Libanius** (314–*c*.393) was a pagan Greek rhetorician from Antioch. He taught at Nicomedia, Constantinople and Antioch. Among his pupils was possibly Ammianus Marcellinus. His works include many speeches and a funeral oration for Julian the Apostate.
  A.F. Norman, *Libanius* (Loeb 1977).

**Marcellinus** (d. *c*.534) spent much of his life at the court in Constantinople. His *Chronicle* is a continuation of Eusebius' *Ecclesiastical History*.
  Comes Marcellinus; Brian Croke; Theodor Mommsen, *The Chronicle of Marcellinus: A Translation and Commentary* (with a reproduction of Mommsen's edition of the text) (Australian Association for Byzantine Studies 1995).

**Martial** (*fl. c.*40–104) wrote twelve books of epigrams, satirizing (among other things) life in Rome.

J. Mitchie, *Martial, The Epigrams* (Penguin 1987).

**Notitia Dignitatum** (*c.*400) is an official index and series of entries for the offices of state and military dispositions in the Roman Empire.

http://www.pvv.ntnu.no/~halsteis/notitia.htm

**Olympiodorus** (before 380–after 425) was a Greek pagan historian from Thebes in Egypt. He wrote memoirs of his life and of the Roman world between 407 and 425. Only fragments of his work survive, although it was summarized by Photius in the ninth century. He was a major source for Zosimus and Sozomen.

R. Blockley, *The Fragmentary Classicising Historians of the Later Roman Empire – Eunapius, Olympiodorus, Priscus and Malchus* II (Text, Translation and Historiographical Notes), ARCA Classical and Medieval Texts, Papers and Monographs 10 (Francis Cairns 1983).

**Orientius of Auch** (*fl.* mid-5th century) was a Gallic Christian convert who became a bishop when Gaul was being overrun by barbarians. His poem, *Commonitorium*, recorded these events in graphic detail.

*Commonitorium* in *Poetae Christiani Minores* (ed R. Ellis), *Corpus Scriptorum Ecclesiasticorum Latinorum* xvi (Vienna 1888).

**Orosius** (late 4th–5th century) was a presbyter from Spain, who in 414 fled from the Vandals to Africa, where he became a pupil of St Augustine. In 415, he prosecuted the British heretic Pelagius in Jerusalem. On Augustine's orders he wrote his *Histories Against the Pagans* (post-*c.*417), which covered all of human history from the beginning of time to 417. It is a vital source for the actual sack of Rome in 410.

http://sites.google.com/site/demontortoise2000/

**Philostorgius** (*c.*368–430/40) was a Cappadocian who lived in Constantinople. He wrote a Church history that continued Eusebius' *Ecclesiastical History* up until 425. His work only survives in a few fragments, but was summarized by Photius. He was a layman and an Arian who provided an alternative history to those written by orthodox historians.

http://www.tertullian.org/fathers/philostorgius.htm

**Photius** (9$^{th}$ century) was twice patriarch of Constantinople (857–67 and 878–86). A prodigious scholar, Photius wrote his *Bibliotheca*, which covered 280 earlier works, and is a vital source for works that have been largely lost, notably those of Olympiodorus and Philostorgius.

http://www.tertullian.org/fathers/photius_01toc.htm

**Procopius** (*c.*500–after 562) was educated in rhetoric and law before serving under Justinian the Great's general Belisarius in Persia, Africa and Italy. His *History of the Wars of Justinian* (*c.*551–3) makes some observations about the fall of Rome.

H. B. Dewing, *Procopius, History of the Wars* (Loeb 1961).

**Rutilius Namatianus** (late 4$^{th}$–5$^{th}$ century) is the last of the classical Latin poets, writing *On his Voyage Home to Gaul* (*c.*417), a poem about a journey that he took from Rome to Gaul in 416 or 417. He was a pagan who held offices under the emperor Honorius, being prefect of Rome in 414. He provides insights into the sack of Rome and its recovery.

J. W. Duff and A. M. Duff, *Minor Latin Poets* (Loeb 1961).

*Scriptores Historiae Augustae* (? late 4$^{th}$ century) is a collection of biographies of Roman emperors covering the years 117 to 284. Its authorship is uncertain, and it is generally agreed that the work cannot be taken at face value.

A. Birley and A. Birley, *Lives of the Later Caesars* (Penguin 2005).

**Socrates** (*c.*380–*c.*450) was a Christian lawyer from Constantinople who continued the *Ecclesiastical Histories* of Eusebius, taking it from 305 to 439. He used a variety of documents, but relied quite heavily on Rufinus and Athanasius. He was the principle source for Sozomen and Theodoret.

P. Schaff and H. Wace (eds), *Nicene & Post-Nicene Fathers, Second Series*, Vol. 2 (Buffalo, New York: Christian Literature Publishing Co. 1890).

http://www.newadvent.org/fathers/2601.html

**Sozomen** (d. *c.*450) was a Christian lawyer in Constantinople who wrote a *History of the Church* from 324 to 439. He used Socrates for most of the work, although at one stage he relies on Olympiodorus.

http://www.freewebs.com/vitaphone1/history/sozomen.html

**Synesius** (*c.*373–*c.*414) was born at Ptolemais in Cyrenaica (eastern Libya). He spent time studying philosophy at Alexandria and was sent on a diplomatic mission to the imperial court at Constantinople. In around 410 he was made bishop of Ptolemais. He wrote a wide selection of Christian and Neo-Platonic works, which give insights into life in the eastern empire during the period of barbarian invasions.

www.livius.org/su-sz/synesius

**Theodoret** (*c.*393–466) became bishop of Cyrrhus (Synia) in 423. He was involved in Christian controversies and even attended the Council of Chalcedon in 451. His *Church History* (post-428) covers the period from Constantine I to 428, and is an important source along with his letters.

http://www.ccel.org/ccel/schaff/npnf203.toc.html

***Theodosian Code*** (438), published in Constantinople, was a collection of laws from the time of Constantine I. The *Code* is vital for understanding the political, economic and social nature of the late Roman Empire.

http://ancientrome.ru/ius/library/codex/theod/tituli.htm (in Latin)

**Virgil** (70–19 BC), was perhaps the greatest and most influential of all Roman poets. His works include *The Aeneid* (*c.*29–19 BC), an epic exploring the foundation of Rome by Trojan refugees under Aeneas, and *The Eclogues* (45–37 BC), a series of pastoral idylls. He was much quoted in later centuries by theologians, including St Jerome.

D. West, *The Aeneid* (Penguin 2003).

**Zosimus, Count** (late 5th century) was a Greek historian who was an advocate of the imperial treasury. He wrote a *New History* (post-410), which covered the Roman Empire from the reign of Augustus to the eve of the sack of Rome in 410. He based his work on three earlier histories written by Dexippus (*fl.* 260), Eunapius and Olympiodorus, whose works only survive in fragments. Zosimus was a strident pagan who saw the rejection of the old gods as the reason for the fall of Rome. He is the most important source for the period 395–410 but, tantalizingly, he breaks off his text just before Alaric sacks Rome.

*Zosimus, New History* (trans. R. T. Ridley), Australian Association for Byzantine Studies, *Byzantina Australiensia* 2 (University of Sydney 1982).

# Further reading

## The Later Roman Empire

A. E. R. Boak, *Manpower Shortage and the Fall of the Roman Empire in the West* (University of Michigan Press 1955)

P. Brown, *The World of Late Antiquity* (Thames and Hudson 1971)

A. Cameron, *The Later Roman Empire* (Fontana 1993)

E. Gibbon, *The Decline and Fall of the Roman Empire* (1776–88)

A. Goldsworthy, *How Rome Fell* (Yale University Press 2009)

P. Heather, *The Fall of the Roman Empire* (Macmillan 2005)

A.H.M. Jones, *Later Roman Empire* (Oxford 1964)

A.H.M. Jones, *The Decline of the Ancient World* (Longmans 1966)

C. Kelly, *Ruling the Roman Empire* (Harvard University Press 2004)

E. J. Kennedy, *The Cambridge History of Classical Literature,* Vol. 5, *The Later Principate* (Cambridge University Press 1982)

H. Lejdegård, *Honorius and the City of Rome* (Uppsala University 2002)

J O'Donnell, *The Ruin of the Roman Empire* (Profile 2009)

J.M. O'Flynn, *Generalissimos of the Western Roman Empire* (University of Alberta Press 1983)

R. Reece, *The Later Roman Empire: An Archaeology AD 150–600* (Tempus 1999)

K.M. Ringrose, *The Perfect Servant – Eunuchs and the Social Construction of Gender in Byzantium* (University of Chicago Press 2003)

E. Swift, *The End of the Western Roman Empire* (Tempus 2000)

J.Vogt, *The Decline of Rome* (Weidenfeld 1967)

B. Ward-Perkins, *The Fall of Rome* (Oxford University Press 2005)

## Constantine and Early Christianity

P. Brown, *Augustine of Hippo* (University of California 1967)

H. Dörres, *Constantine the Great* (Harper 1972)

C. Freeman, *AD 381, Heretics, Pagans and the Christian State* (Pimlico 2009)

E. Hartley, J. Hawkes and M. Henig (eds), *Constantine the Great, York's Roman Emperor* (York Museums and Gallery Trust 2006)

D. Janes, *Romans and Christians* (Tempus 2002)

A.H.M. Jones, *Constantine and the Conversion of Europe* (Macmillan 1948)

R. MacMullen, *The Second Church, Popular Christianity, AD 200–400* (Society of Biblical Literature 2009)

C.M. Odahl, *Constantine and the Christian Empire* (Routledge 2004)

H.A. Pohlsander, *The Emperor Constantine* (Routledge 1996)

## Barbarians and Early Medieval History

A. Barbero, *The Day of the Barbarians* (Atlantic 2007)

R.H.C. Davis, *A History of Medieval Europe* (3rd edition, Longman 2005)

I.M. Ferris, *Enemies of Rome, Barbarians through Roman Eyes* (Sutton 2000)

R. Fossier (ed.), *The Cambridge Illustrated History of the Middle Ages, 350–950* (University of Cambridge 1989)

L. Musset, *The Germanic Invasions, the Making of Europe, AD 400–600* (Pennsylvania State University Press 1975)

L. Webster and M. Brown, *The Transformation of the Roman World, AD 400–900* (British Museum Press 1997)

C. Wickham, *The Inheritance of Rome, A History of Europe* (Allen Lane 2009)

## Rome, Ravenna and Italy

G. Bovini, *Ravenna, Mosaics and Monuments* (A. Longo Editore snc 2008)

R. Krautheimer, *Three Christian Capitals, Topography and Politics: Rome, Constantinople and Milan* (University of California 1983)

B. Lançon, *Rome in Late Antiquity* (Edinburgh University Press 2000)

A. Macadam, *Rome* (Blue Guide 2006)

P. Matyszak, *Ancient Rome on Five Denarii a Day* (Thames & Hudson 2007)

I.D. Portella, *Subterranean Rome* (Könemann 1999)

T.W. Potter, *Roman Italy* (British Museum 1987)

*Ravenna, City of Art* (Editions Salbaroli-Ravenna 2009)

As AD 410 traditionally marks the end of Roman Britain, see also:

## End of Roman Britain

S. Esmonde-Cleary, *The Ending of Roman Britain* (Routledge 1989)

K.R. Dark, *Britain and the End of the Roman Empire* (Tempus 2000)

N. Faulkner, *The Decline and Fall of Roman Britain* (Tempus 2004)

M. Jones, *The End of Roman Britain* (Cornell University Press 1998)

# Endnotes

1   Claudian, *Panegyric on Honorius' VIth Consulship* 39–52ff.
2   Ammianus, *Histories* XVI.10.6ff.
3   Writing in the late 380s, the pagan Libanius laments their sorry state in his speech, 'On Behalf of the Temples'.
4   Claudian, *Panegyric on Honorius' VIth Consulship* 520ff.
5   Claudian, *Stilicho's Consulship* III.234–6.
6   Gibbon, *The Decline and Fall of the Roman Empire* XXXI, following Ammianus, *Histories* XIV.6.9 and XXVIII.4.18.
7   Ibid.
8   Jerome, Epistle 127.
9   Lançon, *Rome in Late Antiquity* 15.
10  Juvenal, *Satire* III.194ff.
11  In the late Roman period, Portus had largely superseded Ostia as the main port of Rome.
12  Ammianus, *Histories* XIV.6.1.
13  Ibid. XIV.6.25–6.
14  The closing of the doors of the Temple of Janus, the double-faced god of gates and doorways, was a sign of peace.
15  Claudian, *Panegyric on Honorius' VIth Consulship* 611ff.
16  Ausonius, *Catalogue of Famous Cities* 1.
17  'Raising to the purple' means being declared emperor.
18  It is notoriously difficult to assess the strength of the late Roman army, as the size of individual units was drastically reduced from that of earlier centuries.
19  John the Lydian, *On the Magistracies of the Roman State* III.65.
20  Zosimus, *New History* IV.41.1, referring to an incident in 387.
21  Lactantius, *On the Deaths of the Persecutors* X.6–11; Eusebius, *Life of Constantine* II.50.
22  There is some doubt as to the exact location of this ceremony. Some suggest it may have been delayed to allow it to take place at the then imperial capital of Trier. However, given the likely presence of the army in Britain's proclamation of Constantine as emperor, it is equally possible that the event took place in York.
23  Eusebius, *Life of Constantine* II.49–52.

24  Ibid. 1.28.

25  The Greek word is *ikon*.

26  Eusebius, op. cit. 1.31.

27  Throughout its history, Rome was able to assimilate elements of foreign religions in a process of so-called syncretism.

28  Apart from certain elements, such as the Immaculate Conception.

29  This was dedicated by the Greeks at Delphi to commemorate their victory over the Persians at the Battle of Plataea in 479 BC.

30  The dispute came to be known as the 'Donatist' Controversy. The Donatists broke away from the Orthodox Church, as they believed that the Orthodox priests who had handed over sacred texts during the Persecutions should be barred from office.

31  Letter of Constantine to Aelafius, 306.

32  Ammianus Marcellinus, *Histories* XXXI.2.2ff.

33  Ibid. XXXI.2.7f.

34  Also known by authors of the time as Scythians and Getae.

35  Eunapius, fr. 37.

36  Ammianus Marcellinus, *Histories* XXXI.4.4.

37  Ibid. XXXI.4.11.

38  Ibid. XXXI.6.4.

39  Ibid. XXXI.12.6.

40  About 13 km.

41  Ammianus Marcellinus, op. cit. XXXI.13.1.

42  Valens was reputedly burned to death with his bodyguard in the tower of a farmhouse: Ammianus Marcellinus, ibid. XXXI.13.12 ff.

43  Ammianus Marcellinus ibid. XXXI.10.19.

44  Theodoret, *Church History* 5.17.

45  Zosimus, *New History* V.3.3–5.

46  Claudian, *Epithalamion on the Marriage of Honorius and Maria* 1–4; 20–2.

47  Jordanes, *The Origin and Deeds of the Getae* 146–7.

48  Zosimus, op. cit. V.5.5–7.

49  Ibid. V.7.5–6.

50  Eunapius, 65.2.1–2.

51  Eunapius, fr. 897.

52  Claudian, *Against Eutropius* 110ff.

53  Zosimus, *New History* V.10.4; 11.1.

54  It seems that Alaric's people were settled south of the Danube, in the areas of east Illyricum and Dacia, although the precise location is not known.

55  Claudian, *Stilicho's Consulship* 1.325–31.

56  Zosimus, *New History* V.11.4.

57  Ibid. V.12.1.

58  Claudian, *Against Eutropius* II.5–6.

59   Zosimus, op. cit. v.24.1–2.
60   Claudian, *On the Gothic War*, 481–4.
61   Ibid. 544–9.25
62   Jordanes, *The Origin and Deeds of the Getae* 148 ff.
63   Claudian, *Panegyric on Honorius' VIth Consulship* 560ff.
64   Orientius, *Commonitorium* II.179–184.
65   Zosimus, *New History* v.31.5.
66   Ibid. v.32.1–2.
67   Ibid. v.32.5.
68   Ibid. v.33.2.
69   The portrait in the Museo Civico Cristiano, Brescia, is not now considered to be Galla Placidia.
70   Zosimus, *New History* v.40.
71   Olympiodorus, fr 4; Procopius, *History of the Wars of Justinian* III.2.27.
72   Jerome, Letter to Principia 1.121.
73   Zosimus, *New History* v. 40.3.
74   Ibid. v.41.
75   Ibid. v.45.
76   Sozomen, *History of the Church* IX.7.
77   Zosimus, op. cit. v.50.2–3.
78   Synesius, *On Kingship* 15.
79   See *figs* 2.5, 3.4 and 5.2. It subsequently became the gesture of benediction in the Christian Church.
80   Sozomen, *History of the Church* IX.8.
81   Zosimus, *New History* VI.7.
82   Sozomen, op.cit. IX.8.
83   With the possible exception of the Anicii who, Zosimus reports, were disconcerted by the prospect of general prosperity.
84   Philostorgius, *Ecclesiastical History* XII.3.
85   Photius, Bibl. Cod. 80, 170.
86   Lejdegård, *Honorius and the City of Rome* 141ff.
87   Ironically, Attalus was to have the fingers of his own right hand hacked off by Honorius before being banished to his own desert island only six years later.
88   Photius, loc. cit.
89   Heather, *The Fall of the Roman Empire* 474.
90   Some authorities date the sack to 20 August.
91   The siege of Troy by the ancient Greeks, who tricked the Trojans into opening their gates to a giant wooden horse concealing the deadly enemy.
92   Procopius, *History of the Wars of Justinian* III.ii.7–39.
93   Orosius, *Histories against the Pagans* 1.vii.
94   Gibbon, 3.xxxi.

95 Sozomen, *History of the Church* 1.9.10.

96 Jerome, Epistle 127.13.

97 Augustine, *City of God* 1.7 ff.

98 Jerome, Epistle 130.

99 Zosimus, *New History* v.5.

100 Gibbon, op.cit. 3.xxxi.

101 Rutilius, *On his Voyage Home to Gaul* 1.331.

102 Quoting Virgil, *Aeneid* x.79.

103 Jerome, Epistle to Demetrias 130.7.

104 Orosius, *Histories against the Pagans* vii.39.

105 Jordanes, *On the Origins and Deeds of the Goths* xxx.156.

106 Ibid. xxx.158.

107 Procopius, *History of the Wars of Justinian* iii.

108 Jordanes, *On the Origins and Deeds of the Goths* xxx.

109 Ibid. xxxi.

110 Not to be confused with the earlier emperors Constantius i and ii.

111 Orosius, *Histories against the Pagans* vii.43.4–6.

112 It is uncertain whether by now Galla Placidia was staying with the Goths of her own volition rather than as a hostage.

113 Bibl. Cod. 80, p. 177; Olympiodorus, fr. 24.

114 Unfortunately the text is corrupt here, and 'thumb' is a conjecture.

115 Olympiodorus, fr. 26; Philostorgius, *Ecclesiastical History* xii.5.2.

116 Bibl Cod. 80, p. 176; Olympiodorus, fr. 26.

117 Bibl. Cod. 80, pp. 174ff.; Olympiodorus, fr. 23.

118 Rutilius, *On his Voyage Home to Gaul*, i. 49.

119 Augustine, Sermon 296.

120 In his Commentary on Ezekiel, Preface to Book i.

121 'According to the scheme of the work that I have undertaken and as the situation requires, I must speak too of the earthly city, a city which, although it is the mistress of the world, is itself ruled by its desire to rule. For it is to this earthly city that those enemies belong, against whom I must defend God's City.' Augustine, *City of God*, Book i, preface.

122 Included in the Vandals' loot were the treasures taken from Jerusalem during the sack of 70, an episode depicted and still visible today on the Arch of Titus in the Roman Forum.

123 Romulus Augustulus' predecessor, Julius Nepos – although living in exile in Dalmatia – was technically still emperor until his death in 480.

124 Eunapius, 55.5–9.

# Timeline 753 BC–AD 711

**BC**

| | |
|---|---|
| 753 | Legendary foundation of Rome |
| 102–1 | Marius defeats the Germanic tribes of Teutones and Cimbri |
| 27 BC–AD 14 | Augustus, first emperor of Rome |

**AD**

| | |
|---|---|
| 9 | Rome loses three legions to the Germans at the Battle of the Teutoburger Forest |
| c.30 | Crucifixion of Christ |
| 177–80 | Rome defeats the Marcomanni and Sarmatian barbarians on the Danube frontier |
| 260–80 | Serious barbarian invasions over the River Rhine, River Danube and in the east |
| 284–305 | Diocletian emperor |
| 303 | Beginning of the Great Persecution of Christians |
| 306–37 | Constantine I emperor |
| 312 | Battle of the Milvian Bridge |
| 313 | 'Edict of Toleration' issued in Milan |
| 325 | Council of Nicaea |
| 330 | Dedication of Constantinople |
| c.350 | Huns defeat Alans and Goths by the River Don, north of the Black Sea |
| 357 | Julian defeats the Alamanni |
| 364–75 | Valentinian I spends much time campaigning against the Alamanni |
| 374–95 | Ambrose, bishop of Milan |
| 376 | Goths cross the Danube |
| 378 | Valens defeated and killed by Goths at the Battle of Hadrianople |

| | |
|---|---|
| 379–95 | Theodosius I emperor |
| 382 | Treaty made with the Goths who settle in the Balkans |
| | Altar of Victory removed from the Senate |
| 390 | Massacre at Thessalonica causes Ambrose to ban Theodosius I from the sacrament of Holy Communion |
| 391 | Theodosius I bans all pagan practices |
| 394 | Theodosius I, with Stilicho and Alaric, defeats Eugenius at the Battle of the River Frigidus |
| 395 | Theodosius dies; empire split east and west between Honorius (west: 395–423) and Arcadius (east: 395–408) |
| 394–5 | Rufinus rules for Arcadius in the east |
| 395–408 | Stilicho *generalissimo* in the west |
| 395–430 | Augustine, bishop of Hippo |
| 395–7 | Alaric's revolt in the Balkans |
| 395–9 | Eutropius rules for Arcadius in the east |
| 397–8 | Gildo's revolt in Africa |
| 398 | Honorius marries Stilicho's daughter, Maria |
| 400 | Gainas briefly occupies Constantinople |
| 401–3 | Alaric invades Italy; Battles of Pollentia and Verona |
| c.402 | Death of Symmachus |
| 404 | Triumph of Honorius in Rome |
| 405–6 | Radagaisus invades Italy; defeated by Stilicho |
| 406 | Alans, Suevi, Vandals and Burgundians cross the Rhine on New Year's Eve |
| 407–11 | Constantine III, usurper in the west |
| 407 | Campaign against the east by Stilicho and Alaric aborted; Maria dies |
| **408** | |
| | Honorius marries Stilicho's second daughter, Thermantia |
| 1 May | Death of Arcadius |
| 13 Aug | Rising against Stilicho's senior allies at Ticinum |
| 22 Aug | Death of Stilicho; subsequent purge of his followers |
| Oct | Alaric invades Italy and besieges Rome |
| c.Nov | Execution of Serena by the Roman Senate |
| c.Nov | The city prefect Pompeianus and Pope Innocent consider pagan sacrifice |

| | |
|---|---|
| *c.*Nov | Alaric demands gold, silver, silk and pepper |
| Dec | Alaric retires to Tuscany |
| Dec | Many slaves (40,000) flee Rome to Alaric |
| Dec | Rome replenishes supplies from Ostia/Portus |
| Dec | Honorius (at Ravenna) made consul for the eighth time |
| Dec | Honorius sends imperial robes to Constantine III at Arles |

**409**

| | |
|---|---|
| Jan | Priscus Attalus and others conduct Rome's first mission to Ravenna, but fail to persuade Honorius to negotiate with Alaric |
| | Valens loses most of his 6,000 men in attacking Alaric |
| | Ataulf arrives in Italy to aid Alaric; suffers some casualties to Olympius |
| | Olympius removed from office in Ravenna |
| | Honorius makes Generidus a general |
| | Jovius' attempts to make terms with Alaric thwarted by Ravenna |
| | Honorius vows not to make peace with Alaric |
| | Alaric repents of the march on Rome and asks just for land in Noricum |
| | Honorius rejects Alaric's demands; Alaric marches on Rome |
| 3 Nov | Priscus Attalus declared emperor at Rome |

**410**

| | |
|---|---|
| | Honorius saved from Attalus and Jovius by the arrival of 4,000 troops from the east |
| | Attalus fails to take Africa; Rome begins to starve |
| *c.*July | Alaric deposes Attalus |
| | Sarus' Goths (on Honorius' side) attack Alaric |
| 24 Aug | Alaric sacks Rome |
| late Aug | The Goths head south to sack Capua and Nola |
| ? Sep | The Goths fail to sail to North Africa |

| | |
|---|---|
| 410–11 | Alaric dies at Consentia |
| | Ataulf succeeds Alaric |
| 411 | Ataulf leads the Goths north, via Rome again, to Gaul; fall of Constantine III |

| | |
|---|---|
| 411–13 | Jovinus, usurper in Gaul |
| 412–14 | Senate offices and Baths of Sura (Aventine) restored |
| 413 and 418 | Tax remissions made to cities in central and south Italy after Gothic invasion |
| 413 | Heraclian, count of Africa, rebels and is defeated |
| 413–26 | Augustine writes *The City of God* |
| 414 | Marriage of Ataulf to Galla Placidia |
| 414–15 | Second reign of Priscus Attalus |
| 415 | Assassination of Ataulf; Galla Placidia returned to Ravenna |
| ?416 | Basilica Julia restored in the Roman Forum |
| 417 | Galla Placidia marries Constantius |
| 418 | Visigoths settle in Aquitaine |
| 421 | Constantius III declared emperor |
| 423 | Death of Honorius |
| 425–55 | Valentinian III (son of Galla Placidia) emperor of the west |
| 430 | Death of Augustine at Hippo |
| 438 | *Theodosian Code* written |
| 439 | Vandals take Carthage |
| 446–53 | Attila ruler of the Huns |
| 450 | Death of Galla Placidia |
| 451 | Huns defeated at the Battle of the Catalaunian Fields |
| 455 | Rome sacked by the Vandals |
| 472 | Rome sacked by Ricimer |
| 476 | Romulus Augustulus deposed by Odovacer; effective end of the western empire |
| 476–93 | Odovacer, king of Italy |
| 480 | Julius Nepos, last official emperor of the west, dies |
| 493–526 | Theodoric the Ostrogoth, king of Italy |
| 535–52 | War in Italy between the Ostrogoths and Byzantine Empire |
| 547 | Rome sacked by Totila the Ostrogoth after siege |
| 568 | Lombards conquer Italy |
| 590–604 | Pope Gregory the Great |
| 711 | Visigothic Kingdom of Spain conquered by the Umayyads |

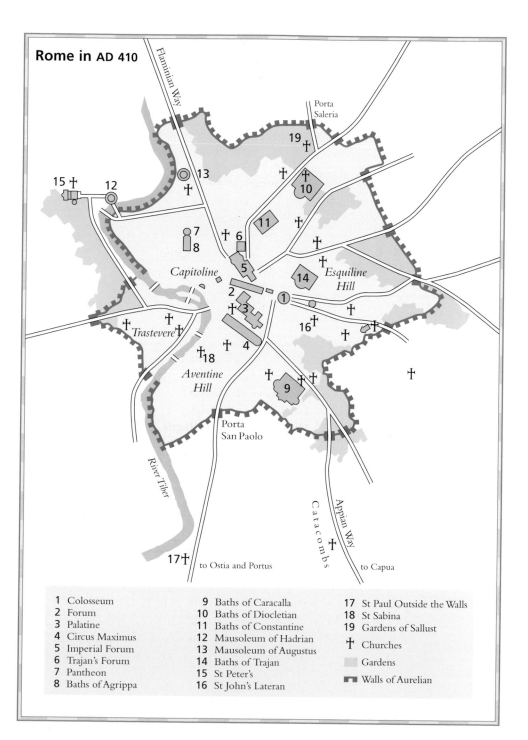

# Rome in AD 410

Porta
Saleria

15 🕇    12

13

19 🕇

🕇   🕇
10

11   🕇

7
8    🕇   6

🕇

*Capitoline*

5

🕇 14   *Esquiline Hill*

2
🕇 3
🕇   🕇   *Trastevere* 🕇    1

16 🕇

🕇

🕇   🕇    4

🕇

🕇 18

*Aventine Hill*

🕇   🕇   🕇

9

Porta
San Paolo

*River Tiber*

17 🕇   to Ostia and Portus

*Flaminian Way*

*Catacombs*

*Appian Way*

to Capua

| | | |
|---|---|---|
| 1 Colosseum | 9 Baths of Caracalla | 17 St Paul Outside the Walls |
| 2 Forum | 10 Baths of Diocletian | 18 St Sabina |
| 3 Palatine | 11 Baths of Constantine | 19 Gardens of Sallust |
| 4 Circus Maximus | 12 Mausoleum of Hadrian | 🕇 Churches |
| 5 Imperial Forum | 13 Mausoleum of Augustus | Gardens |
| 6 Trajan's Forum | 14 Baths of Trajan | Walls of Aurelian |
| 7 Pantheon | 15 St Peter's | |
| 8 Baths of Agrippa | 16 St John's Lateran | |

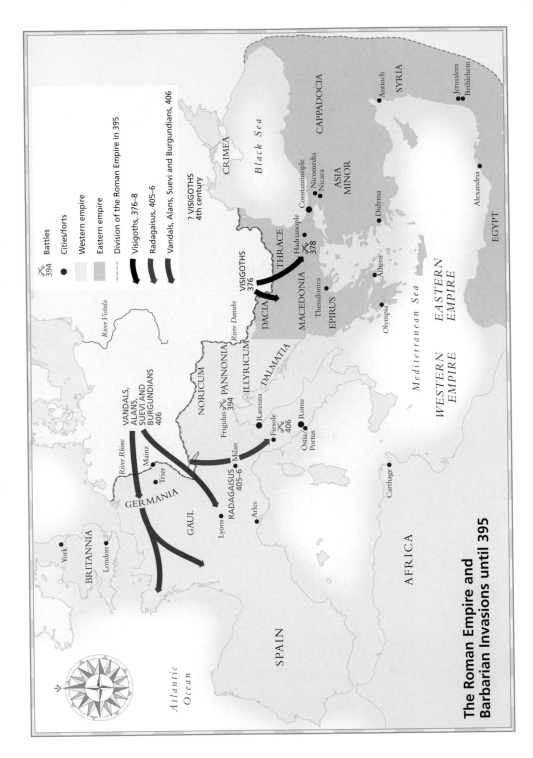

The Roman Empire and Barbarian Invasions until 395

**Legend:**

Battles — 394

Cities/forts — ●

Western empire

Eastern empire

Division of the Roman Empire in 395

Visigoths, 376–8

Radagaisus, 405–6

Vandals, Alans, Suevi and Burgundians, 406

**Map labels:**

Atlantic Ocean

BRITANNIA — York, London

GERMANIA — River Rhine, Mainz, Trier

GAUL — Lyons, Arles

SPAIN

AFRICA — Carthage

RADAGAISUS 405–6, Milan

VANDALS, ALANS, SUEVI AND BURGUNDIANS 406

NORICUM — Frigidus 394, PANNONIA

ILLYRICUM

DALMATIA

Ravenna, Fiesole 406, Rome, Ostia, Portus

River Danube, River Vistula

DACIA, VISIGOTHS 376

? VISIGOTHS 4th century

MACEDONIA — Thessalonica

EPIRUS, THRACE, Hadrianople 378

Olympia, Athens

CRIMEA, Black Sea

Constantinople, Nicomedia, Nicaea

CAPPADOCIA

ASIA MINOR — Didyma

SYRIA — Antioch

Jerusalem, Bethlehem

Alexandria

EGYPT

Mediterranean Sea

WESTERN EMPIRE

EASTERN EMPIRE

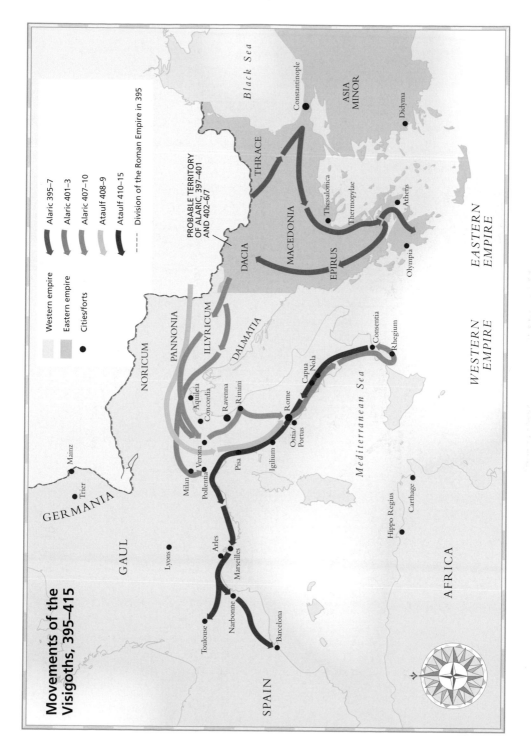

# Movements of the
Visigoths, 395–415

Alaric 395–7
Alaric 401–3
Alaric 407–10
Ataulf 408–9
Ataulf 410–15
Division of the Roman Empire in 395

Western empire
Eastern empire
Cities/forts

PROBABLE TERRITORY
OF ALARIC, 397–401
AND 402–6/7

*Black Sea*

ASIA
MINOR

Didyma

THRACE

Constantinople

MACEDONIA

Thessalonica
Thermopylae

Athens

EPIRUS

Olympia

EASTERN
EMPIRE

DACIA

PANNONIA

NORICUM

ILLYRICUM

DALMATIA

Aquileia
Concordia
Ravenna
Rimini

Verona
Pollentia
Milan

Consentia
Rhegium

Capua
Nola

Rome

Ostia
Portus

Pisa
Igilium

*Mediterranean Sea*

WESTERN
EMPIRE

Hippo Regius
Carthage

GERMANIA

Mainz
Trier

GAUL

Lyons

Arles
Marseilles

Narbonne

Toulouse

Barcelona

SPAIN

AFRICA

# Index

*Page numbers in italics refer to illustrations and their captions.*

Adriatic Sea 80
Aelafius 47
Aelia Eudoxia *See* Eudoxia
Aemilia 120
Africa 14, 25, 36, 42, 44–5, 47, 74, 93, *96*, 99, 115, *116*, 117, *119*, 119–20, 122, 132–4, 140–1, *146*, 147, 150, 152, 153, 156–60, 166–7, 176–8, *180–1*
Alamanni 61, 175
Alans 85, 139, 157, 175–6, *180*
Alaric 13, 16, 28, 32, 48, 51, 65–6, 69–70, 73–74, 79, 82–3, *83*, 84–8, 93–4, 97–101, 104–6, 108–111, 113–120, *120*, 122–5 *125–6*, 126–9, 131, *134*, 136, 138, *146*, 153, 156–160, 162, 168, 176–7, *181*
Albania 71
Alexandria 16, 25, *46*, 51, 163, 168, *180*
Alps 79, 82, 84, 103, 107, 139
Altar of Victory 50, 74, 100, *113*, 160, 176
Ambrose (St) 50–1, *51*, 65, 74, *113*, 147, 161, 163, 175–6
Ammianus Marcellinus *17*, 17–9, 21, 26, 54, *55*, 58, 163, 165
Anastasius 151
Anicii 22, 125
Antioch 17, 26, 33, 37, *46*, 163, *180*
Antiochus 70
Antony (St) 49
Apennines 95, 102
Apollo 37, 46
Appian Way 134, *134*, *179*
Aquileia 94, 164, *181*
Arcadia 71
Arcadius 66–8, *68–9*, 70, 72, 76–7, 84, 88, 153, 155–6, 160–1, 176
Arians 48, 52, 58, 114, 161, 164, 166
Ariminum *See* Rimini
Aristotle 56
Arius 48
Arles 139, 154, 177, *180–1*
Ataulf 93, 106–8, 114, 138–44, 153–4, 156–7, 159–60, 177–8, *181*
Athanaric 70
Attalus *see* Priscus Attalus
Attila 149, 154, 156, 159, 178
Augusta (title) 77, 144
Augustine of Hippo (St) 14, 131, 147–8, *148*, 159, 163, 166, 176, 178
Augustine of Canterbury (St) 152

Augustus (Gaius Julius) 19, 80–1, 126, *126*, 140, 168, 175
Augustus (title) 39, 64, 83
Aventine Hill 22, 49, *49*, 129, 144, 158, 178, *179*
Bacchus 83
*Bagaudae* 35
Balkans 61, 64
Barbarian 12–3, 16, 30–31, *31*, 32–33, 35–6, 54, *55*, 56–9, 61, *61*, 63, 65–6, 71, 76, 78, *83*, 83–6, 88–90, 93, 99, 101–2, *105*, 107, 109–11, 116–7, 119, 123–4, 129, 131, 149, 150, 152
Barcelona 142, *181*
Basilica Julia 144, *145*, 178
Bath 31
Bathanarius 76, 93
Baths of Sura 144, 178
Belisarius *146*, 151–2, 158, 167
Bethlehem 140, 147, 156, 164, 180
Black Sea 57, 175, *180–1*
Boeotia 71
Boethius 151, 161
Bologna 89–90
Bordeaux 49, 139, 163
Bosphorus 71
Britain 34, *35*, *37*, 39–40, 65, 82, *85*, 85–6, 120, 150, 154, 158, *180*
Burgundii 85, 139, 157, 176, *180*
Busentus 136
Caecilianus 104
Caesar (Gaius Julius) 21, 28, *113*
Caesar (title) 33, 37, 40
Caesarea (Ravenna) 81
Capitol *17*, 98, 145, 150, *179*
Cappadocia 57, *180*
Capua 134, *134*, 177, *179–80*
Carthage 42, *115*, 116–7, 119, *119*, 121, 139–40, 145, *146*, 147, 150–1, 156–7, 163, 178, *180–1*
Cassiodorus 151, 161
Chariot 21, 26–7, *27*, 84, *121*, 145
Charioteer 26, 50, 65
China 20
Christ 22, 41–2, *42*, 43–4, 46, 48–9, 51, *129*, 131, 157–8, 175
Christianity 13, 19, 22, 37–8, 40–1, *42–3*, 43–4, 46–7, 51–2, 54, 58, *75*, 97, 147, 152, 156–8, 161, 163, 165
Christians 12–4, 20, 37–8, 40, 43, 45, *45*, 48, *49*, 50–1, 57, 61, 82, 85, *90*, *98*, *102*, 107, 127–9, 131–2, 147, 154, 156, 175
Church (institution) 22, 41, 45, 47–50, 93, 97–8, 127, 155
Circus 26–7, *64*, 65, 80
Circus Maximus 27, *27*, 115, *115*, 121, *121*, 145, 179
Classe *80*, 81

Claudian 16–7, 19–20, 27, 30, 69, 73, 76–9, 83, 92, 96, *116*, *119*, 163–4
Colosseum *16*, 19, *19*, 26, 138, 144, 151, *179*
Concordia 94, *181*
Consentia 136, 177, *181*
Constans (envoy) 116–7, 119
Constantine I 13, 38–42, *42–3*, 43–4, *44*, 45–8, 52, 57, 74, 114, 154, 156, 158, 164–5, 168, 174
Constantine III *84*, 86–9, 103, *105*, 108, 112, 117, 120, 139–40, 154, 160, 176–8
Constantinople 25, *46*, 46–7, 52, 61, *64*, 67, *68–9*, 70–1, *71*, 72–4, 77, 86, 88, 102, *116*, 118, 150, 153–4, 156, 158–61, 165–8, 175–6, *180–1*
Constantius I 38–40, *40*, 154
Constantius II *17*, 17–8, 48, 52, 154
Constantius III 139–141, 143–4, 154, 156, 159, 162, 178
Corn and grain supply 25, *37*, 96, *96*, 110, 115, *116*, 117, *119*, 132, 140, 157
Cremona 94
Croatia 33, *61*
Cyprus 77, 155
Dacia 57, 73, *180–1*
Dalmatia *45*, 104, 106–8, 110, *180–1*
Danube 31, 54, *55*, 56–9, 64, 70, 77, 80, 82, 84, 93, 110, 155, 159, 165, 175, *180*
Delphi 46
Demetrias 131–2
Didyma 37, *180–1*
Diocletian 13, *30*, 32, *32*, *33*, 33, 34–41, 47, 49, *113*, 154–6, 164–5, 175
'Edict of Toleration' 43, 154, 175
Egypt 16, 30, *31*, 44, 46, 48–9, 51, *96*, 114, *116*, 166, *180*
Eleusinian Mysteries 50
English Channel 86
Epirus 71, 108, *180–1*
Eucherius 27, *78*, 89, 92–3, 95, 145, 155–6, 160
Eudocia 150, 159
Eudoxia 68, *69*, 77, 155
Eugenius 51–2, 74, 153, 155, 160, 162, 176
Eunapius 14, 56, 67, 79, 152, 164, 168
Eunuch 34, 67, 72–3, 77, 88, 92–3, 106, *107*, 118, 138, 140, 151, 155–6, 158–9
Euphrates 50
Eusebius (Church Father) 39, 41–2, 164–7